MIND-FULL
DETOX

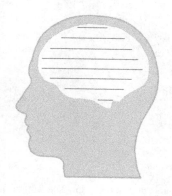

MIND-FULL
DETOX

Grief Journal Experience

Yadle Regnier

XULON PRESS

Xulon Press
2301 Lucien Way #415
Maitland, FL 32751
407.339.4217
www.xulonpress.com

Paperback ISBN-13: 978-1-66282-592-7
Ebook ISBN-13: 978-1-66282-593-4

This book is dedicated to the people who are seeking emotional healing and those who are supporting their friends and families that are going through the process of healing.

TABLE OF CONTENTS

INTRODUCTION

I always hear the phrase "It is time to heal" about emotional healing. Hearing that phrase can either go way over a person's head or be overwhelming due to a lack of guidance and instructions. Some people may not know where to start. It's like expecting someone who has never been to an unfamiliar destination to know how to arrive there without an address or instructions on how to reach that destination.

I am not a licensed therapist. This book is simply what I experienced from grief journaling when it was introduced to me by Pastor Kelvin at Nyack College and what the Holy Spirit placed on my heart to help you start the process of emotional healing. I highly encourage you to seek a Christian counselor. I've had great experiences and breakthroughs when I sought counseling. I pray that you will experience your breakthrough, as well.

Even though this book doesn't have many pages, it's not something to read in a short period just so you can check off that you have read a book. I recommend that you take your time to reflect, discover (or rediscover), and examine why you cannot fully receive what God is doing in your life.

First and foremost, I want to thank you for choosing this book to help guide you through emotional healing. I also want to commend you for taking the initiative to walk in freedom. I've been praying and fasting for you. I pray that you will allow yourself to reflect, feel, let go, and have healing conversations with God. In this book, you will find prayers and declarations that will help you as you embark on this emotional healing journey. You will also find an amalgam of reasons that led you to where you are.

I was inspired to write this book based on my experience with a grief journal that my mentor, Pastor Kelvin, suggested I write when I attended Nyack College. After I wrote in my grief journal, I learned so much about myself. I was able to release a lot of events and people that had affected my life. There were certain habits and mindsets that I needed to change. I had to unclutter my mind.

Many people are emotionally unhealthy due to things they've experienced from their childhood or current circumstances. It would be selfish of me not to share this experience and help those who are feeling broken, scared, and insecure like I was. As you embark on this journey to emotional healing, I pray that you will feel the presence of God so strongly that it shakes out the fear of being healed, and that you will find your identity, even through the trauma you've experienced. I am genuinely excited about your outcome.

CLOGGED PIPE

G rab a pen, a journal (the one that's provided for you in the back of this book), and, most importantly, your heart and mind, ready to release the things that have been holding you back. Be prepared for restoration! You may be wondering what you are going to release. Perhaps you've experienced some form of loss (death of a loved one, divorce, job, home, finances, innocence, childhood), disappointment, or betrayal. Regardless of the specifics, you've experienced hurt. Unfortunately, no one is exempt from life's challenges. "The righteous person may have many troubles, but the Lord delivers him from them all" (Ps. 34:19). However, we're fortunate to cast all our cares and burdens on Jesus Christ.

> *Cast your burden upon the Lord and he will sustain you; he will never let the righteous be shaken. (Ps. 55:22)*

OUR HEAVENLY FATHER WANTS TO POUR INTO US

Picture this: You're using a sink. You turn the knob and adjust the water, then you notice the water is not going down the drain. The sink begins to overflow, so you shut the water off to avoid flooding. Now you think, *What could be in this pipe to cause the sink to flood?* Do you see where I'm going with this? Our heavenly Father wants to pour into us, yet we have situations (trauma) from our past, or even present, that hinder us from fully receiving what He has for us.

What to Expect

During the next couple of days, your goal is to dig deep and bring the pain that's hidden in your heart to light. Additionally, you will need to process what you've been through or what you're going through and release it to your Father. As the pain you have endured begins to resurface, you may find yourself feeling uncomfortable. That is entirely reasonable, but it is time to heal and make peace with your past or your current situation as you surrender to God. This journal experience will challenge you to be vulnerable and, most importantly, to feel. So many people believe vulnerability shows weakness; in reality, however, you're making room to receive growth. I dare you to dig deep, search the truth, and face it!

Mind

I am genuinely fascinated with the human mind. It is very complex. Psychologists spend many years studying the human mind and behavior to draw conclusions and theories about the mind. While there have been studies on the human mind, there have also been plans and schemes to destroy it. No, no, no—I'm not talking about psychologists doing something crazy like that. I'm talking about the enemy!

The enemy is also fascinated with the mind. The mind is a battleground, a place where the enemy likes to antagonize, confuse, trap, deceive, and, worst of all, mark as his territory. We can see, from the beginning of time, that he had a field day with Adam and Eve. He deceived Eve and questioned her knowledge, tricking her into believing she wouldn't die if she ate from the forbidden tree. He made that tree desirable enough for her to disobey God. After Adam and Eve ate the fruit, their eyes were opened. They became aware that they were naked, so they sewed together fig leaves and made themselves coverings (see Genesis 7).

Let's take a step back and let that sink in. Man, oh man, haven't we all been there, where we've done something against the will of God and try to patch it, fix it on our own, or hide from Him? The word *covering* from that scripture makes me think of the many things we have attempted to cover from God. We try to cover our shame, trauma, and heart from Him, yet we expect our minds to be at peace.

I can only imagine the shame, guilt, and regret Eve felt as she was leaving the Garden of Eden. I have always wondered if she replayed that conversation with the serpent over and over in her mind. Did that experience affect her communication skills with her husband? Did she carry this experience into every chapter of her life? The enemy knows how to deceive a person so much that he makes that person believe the very opposite of what God speaks into their life. It happened to Eve, and it happened to me!

When I was eight years old, someone I looked up to called me "slow." On several occasions, this person belittled me. That person's action and poor choice of words penetrated my mind. I replayed those words and experiences with that person so many times that it made a negative impact in my life. Since I believed that I was slow, I struggled throughout my entire academic career.

It was so bad that I questioned how I ever made it to college. Whenever I had a paper due, I experienced anxiety. Then, when I had to submit my paper to my professor, I would expect a low grade. The crazy part was that when I placed my paper on my professor's desk, sometimes I thought of taking the assignment back and walking out of the class. But what I really did was sit in my seat and spend my entire time thinking, *Will the professor understand my points? What about my grammar and punctuation? Oh gosh, what did I just submit?* I would prepare my mind for disappointment by choosing lower expectations because I had spent many years believing I couldn't achieve good grades.

The waiting game to get my paper back drove me crazy. I was always afraid to see what grade the professor gave me on my paper. That feeling drained me. Then, when I received my paper, I'd get an A or a B+. *I think the professor made a mistake, but I'll take the grade.* That's the statement I made to myself every time I got a paper back. Do you see how toxic my thoughts were?

This attitude affected all areas of my life. I missed opportunities to allow God to pour into me so I could pour into others because I felt I wasn't good enough. For example, my school had auditions for a worship leader position, but I thought to myself, *That position is way out of my league.* One day, Pastor Kelvin, my campus pastor, approached me and asked, "How come you didn't audition for the worship leader position? I was expecting you to try out." I made up an excuse about taking too many credits for the semester and not having the time to lead worship (sorry, Pastor Kelvin, for lying to you). What I really wanted to say was, "Pastor, I'm just not good enough." I walked away thinking, *How could this man even think I would audition?* This mentality prohibited me from receiving what God could have done through me.

God's Word says, "You are complete in Him, who is the head of all principality of power" (Col. 2:10 NKJV), but the enemy had me believing I wasn't complete. God's Word says, "Beloved, I pray that you may prosper in all things, and be in health, just as your soul prospers" (3 John 1:2 NKJV), but the enemy had me thinking I would not prosper in school. God's Word says, "Do not remember former things nor consider the things of old" (Isa. 43:18 NKJV), yet the enemy had me replaying those lies from my past. I spent many years thinking the opposite of what God's Word says about me. This experience warranted me to let God have His way so I could heal through journaling.

You're probably wondering how I managed to write an entire book. Well, let's just say I had to lean unto God's understanding instead of mine. This book is actually a testament of overcoming my anxiety of writing. It is a result of my mental and emotional detox journey. See, I believe this book was already written before I was born. God knew that I'd have encounters with people who would affect my mind, but something had to get done. Once I made the decision to allow Him to detox what was harming my mind and future, an abundance of healing and blessings took place.

After I wrote in my grief journal for the first time, I began to see the results of God removing my negative way of thinking about my writing ability. During my senior year of college, I had to write a thirty-page paper on my major. This time around, though, my anxiety wasn't as strong as usual. I remember praying and asking God to prepare me and to give my mind peace. I wrote the paper without my mind attacking me; in fact, after writing the thirty-page paper, I remember saying I had enjoyed the process. Then I heard God say, *You'll be writing books in the future.* I chuckled at what God said, and my response was, *Okay, God, You're funny*.

This is where you can start writing. I hope you have that pen ready. What's your experience? What are some things God's Word says about you that the enemy has you thinking the opposite? Take a few minutes, or as long as you want, and write down all those lies that have been lingering in your mind.

Your mind has reached its capacity to hold on to those lies. It's full! Release those lies.

Hoarder

For the past couple of years, I've had the chance to watch *Hoarding: Buried Alive* on TLC. Hoarding is a disease that is similar to having an addiction. Whenever the hoarders on this show give a tour of their living space to family or friends, there is always a sense of shock, followed by repulsiveness.

Based on my observations, the common element of these hoarders' stories is their experiences with a traumatic past that is stored in their minds; they have never dealt with the underlying issues. While watching this show, I noticed the patients always had a therapist to help them part with possessions of no real value; however, there was always an unwillingness on the part of the hoarders to part with these items. It is easy to judge these people and look at their homes with disgust, but in some ways, we all can relate to them.

You might be holding on to painful feelings, such as fear, abandonment, abuse, betrayal, humiliation, or insignificance. I may not have listed the particular painful feeling you're holding on to, but my question is, are you willing to let go of it? Painful feelings have been stored in your mind and are limiting you from moving forward. You may find yourself dealing with random negative emotions, and based on your experience, you know where these are coming from. Nonetheless, you have chosen to put off dealing with it because it seems much easier and more comfortable to ignore it. However, God wants you to do new things in your life, and He wants you to be free from these painful emotions so you can live the life He has called you to live.

Full

"If you don't allow yourself to grieve over Dad's death, it will be like taking a giant breath in and just holding it there for the rest of your life." This quote is from one of the characters, Kevin, in my favorite television show, *This Is Us* on NBC. After the death of his father, Mr. Pearson, Kevin never allowed himself to grieve. He later found himself addicted to painkillers and alcohol. All of the emotions from his father's death were suppressed inside. Kevin eventually hit rock bottom and had to seek professional help. His twin sister told him he needed to let go and heal from the father's death. Kevin later shared this quote at his sister's wedding as part of his speech.

Although this is a fictional drama, many people have found themselves in Kevin's place, a place where they have experienced some form of loss but haven't grieved. They might find themselves full of toxic emotions, and they are in dire need of taking a moment to relax, take a deep breath, and let it out.

Detox

There are many wellness books and videos on the importance of detoxification of the body. There are guides for a twenty-one-day or even a thirty-day cleanse. Some people detox to get a head start on a weight-loss journey or for health purposes. I myself have done a detox before. I've come across guides that strategically give you foods to eat and foods to avoid, things to drink and not to drink. I am all for doing a detox or cleanse for the body, but I truly believe there has to be a balance. You can't work on your body and not work on your mind and soul. In order to reap the maximum results, you have to work on your mind, body, and soul.

The Change in Me

A couple of years ago, I went on a weight-loss journey. I was overweight and not happy with my body. I spent many years struggling with low self-esteem. I made up my mind to change my diet, and I began to exercise. I started walking, then later jogging, in the mornings. At first, it was a struggle for me; then, eventually, I started running two miles. Gradually, I started running eight miles! I was so proud of myself. I lost over forty pounds, and that was a huge accomplishment for me. I surpassed my weight-loss goal, and I was the thinnest I'd ever been.

These accomplishments were short-lived, however, due to the negative thoughts I entertained. Every time I stared at myself in the mirror, I had a hard time recognizing myself. I didn't like who was staring back at me. I saw a thinner person, yet I didn't feel beautiful. I was so confused. I had thought after losing all the weight, I'd finally feel beautiful, but I thought wrong. I spent those few months working so hard on my body, but not my mind. As my body changed drastically, my mind remained stagnant. As my body went through the process of being renewed, my mind needed the same. The extra weight I carried was gone, yet the poor thoughts of a low self-image weighed heavy on my soul. My mind was in need of a detox; the little girl who struggled with low self-esteem was still in there, and I had to address her and remind her that she was beautiful and fearfully and wonderfully made.

> *Do not conform to the pattern of this world, but be transform by the renewing of your mind.* (Rom. 12:2)

GOD HAS GREAT PLANS FOR YOUR LIFE

Transformation

Have you ever been frustrated but couldn't find the reason for your frustration? Perhaps you think you're just tired or hungry, but after you take a nap or eat something, you still feel frustrated. Although you think it's your body that needs something, chances are, God is tugging at your heart to alert you about the condition of your mind. Your mind needs a renewal, but it requires transformation.

You have probably heard this many times, but God has great plans for your life. However, if you don't transform your current state of mind, you can't accommodate what He has for you. If you're bitter after a breakup or don't love yourself, how can you fully love a future spouse? You've been asking God for a financial breakthrough, but if you don't budget your money wisely and you spend money carelessly, how will you ever see it?

Transformation can be uncomfortable, yet it is rewarding. It may come at a cost; for example, you may lose some close people in your life. Transformation can be a challenge because you may have to break out of routine. All that you've been accustomed to or have aligned yourself with has been embedded in your mind. Take, for instance, a woman who has been working at the same job for the past thirty-eight years. She wakes up at 4:00 a.m. to get ready for work. This woman does not even use an alarm clock to get up because her eyes open naturally at that time. Even when she's on vacation and has the chance to sleep in, her body naturally wakes up without the assistance of an alarm clock. Her mind and body have conformed to the routine of waking up at 4:00 a.m.

You Are What You Feed Your Mind

YOU BECOME WHAT YOU FEED YOUR MIND

"You are what you eat" is a phrase many nutritionists and personal trainers use to emphasize the need to eat healthful food in order to be fit and healthy. I believe this phrase applies to the mind as well: you become what you feed your mind. If you feed your mind doubt and negative thoughts, then you will display doubtful qualities in your life. If you feed your mind with peace and positive thoughts, then you will become a peaceful person. Furthermore, feeding your mind with the Word of God gives you a better understanding of who He is.

Transformation starts internally. God wants to transform your mind, but if you're aligning yourself with the things of this world, there's no room for the necessary internal transformation. When I decided to go on my weight-loss journey, my mind was still conformed to what I thought of myself (ugly). As God began to work on my mind, I had to detach from the people who caused me to think so lowly of myself. With the affirmation and support of close friends I met in college, I began the journey of renewing my mind.

There's no special formula for transformation, but you have to want it for yourself. To start, feed your mind with positivity, and surround yourself with people who will uphold you and not tear you down. You have to renew your mind so it will accommodate the new season and purpose God has for you.

Butterfly

As I wrote about transformation, I had a vision of a butterfly. There is no doubt the butterfly had a significant meaning; it made sense to have that vision because a butterfly goes through a powerful process of transformation (metamorphosis). I believe God wants to transform us, but moving through different life cycles can be uncomfortable and overwhelming.

When we see this delicate creature, we tend to get caught up with its beauty, but do not realize it was once a creature without wings. The butterfly has the ability to go through its important changes with grace, and God wants you to know if a butterfly can go through its essential changes, so—can—you! A butterfly can't skip the caterpillar stage and emerge into the creature that it is intended to be. This is similar to the process of emotional healing. We can't evolve to our fullest potential if we try to skip the process of emotional healing.

Time of Reflection

- The devil tells you the opposite of what God says.
- Are you hoarding painful feelings?
- Are you willing to part with them?
- Can you identify the painful feelings?
- Renew your mind.

  Forget the former things; do not dwell on the past. See, I am doing a new thing! (Isa. 43:18–19)

Heavenly Father,

You want to do new things in Your beloved's life, but there are old things Your beloved is holding on to. Teach Your children how to let go of the things that are keeping them from moving forward. Help them to identify painful feelings, and set their minds free. We thank You for wanting to do something new in the life of Your beloved.

Place your hand over your head and pray the following:

Father,

My mind is Yours; conform it. Renew my mind. Fill my mind with Your goodness. Teach me how to lean on You and not on things of this world. Amen.

If you want to say your prayer aloud, feel free to do so.

2

EMOTIONAL SCAR

My Journal

WHAT I DID WAS I LEARNED TO ADAPT TO THE PAIN, AND I CARRIED IT, THINKING I WAS FINE

As a child growing up, I always kept a diary. Of course, I filled those pages with my crushes, people who hurt my feelings, breakups, or fights I had with my brother. As I grew older, I would go back and skim through some of the pages and laugh at the things I had said or my way of thinking. It was as if the older version of me was facing the younger version of me. Although I saw growth between my old self and the current person, I didn't speak life into the younger me. I recognized that I generally moved on from past hurts without really resolving them. What I did was I learned to adapt to the pain, and I carried it, thinking I was fine.

Bandage

I have several years of experience working with children. One thing I know is that children love bandages. Even if they have just a little "boo-boo," they will ask for a bandage because they have the notion it will make their boo-boo feel better.

One day, I took my four-year-old son on a nature walk, but for him, it was more like a hop-skip-run nature experience. After I had told him for at least twenty times to stop running, jumping, and hopping, he lost his balance and fell on his knees. He began to cry when he saw he had scraped his knees against the pavement. He cried and begged me for a bandage. I explained that I had to clean his boo-boo with alcohol before I could put a bandage on it.

We got home, and he was still crying about his scrape. I sat him down and took out the first-aid kit. I removed alcohol pads, Neosporin, and the "lifesaver," the bandage. I gently placed my son's leg across my lap and warned him that he might feel a little sting from the alcohol. To that, he cried out loud, "No, just put on the Band-Aid." I explained to him why I had to clean the scrape: I didn't want it to get infected. My explanation, however, went in one ear and out the other. The only word he held on to was the word *sting*.

I eventually rubbed the alcohol pad across the scrape and braced my ears against the loud cry coming from my four-year-old. I rubbed on Neosporin and placed the bandage on his scrape. I personally didn't think he needed the bandage, but to a four-year-old, that bandage was a lifesaver.

After a day or two, the adhesive from the bandage wore off and my son asked for another one. This time around, I told him no, to let the wound heal without the Band-Aid. However, he insisted that he needed the Band-Aid. I quickly realized that my son didn't want to see his boo-boo; covering it up was easier to deal with than seeing a scrape on his knee.

In June 2017, my husband fractured his leg. He had three surgeries. Even though the recovery process after any surgery demands a lot of patience, my husband's third surgery took a toll on the family. In this procedure, he had two screws removed, and a couple of weeks after the surgery, he had the stitches removed. Unfortunately, his incision from the surgery became infected. We had to make several trips to the hospital, and my husband was prescribed antibiotics. He was on close watch due to the infection.

During the course of the healing process, my husband's incision was covered by a small gauze pad and a bandage. The doctor suggested that he change the gauze and bandage twice a day due to the drainage. Whenever my husband changed his bandage, I noticed that the incision was always moist. After another doctor's visit, the doctor suggested we let the incision get air, and we noticed a significant change once we did that. The incision began to heal. This made me think about the process of emotional healing.

How many times have you been emotionally hurt and just put a Band-Aid over the wound? When the adhesive begins to wear off, you place a new bandage over the scar that has formed. At this point in your life, if you were to draw the condition of your heart, what would it look like? What bandage are you placing over the scar? It might be a new relationship you know deep down you're not ready for, a new hairstyle, a new location, a new job, or even drugs. There are many other things you can use as a bandage to cover your pain, but all of them are only a temporary fix.

If you don't expose this pain to God, you will find yourself in a never-ending cycle of searching for a temporary fix. "Just put on the Band-Aid!" was my son's plea. Since I am his mother, he knew I had the capability to make him feel better, but he had his own preference as to how I should do this. He didn't trust my process, and he also feared the sting. The alcohol that I rubbed on the scrape did sting, of course, and that was uncomfortable for him, and even for me, but I didn't want his scrape to get infected. I love my son, and I want nothing but the best for him. "For my thoughts are not your thoughts, neither are your ways my ways, declares the Lord" (Isa. 55:8). God has His own way and plans on how He wants to heal you. Don't put limitations on Him.

Superbug

Many of us know that God is capable of healing us emotionally, but we don't want to go through the process, for various reasons. We ask Him for help, but we place our expectations on how He should heal us: "God, heal my heart, but I'm not ready to give this up, or let go of that." If you find yourself saying this, you, my friend, have placed limitations on God. God wants to heal your whole heart, not half of it.

YOU HAVE TO ADDRESS THE UNDER-LYING ISSUE

Rapper Jay-Z had an interview with CNN's news commentator Van Jones. The rapper was explaining his theory of closet racists running back to their holes when a racial issue is addressed poorly. Jay-Z said something profound: "What you've done is spray perfume. What you do when you do that is the bugs come and you create a superbug. You don't take care of the problem; you don't take the trash out; you keep spraying whatever over it to make it acceptable."[1] Although Jay-Z was sharing his theory about racism, his explanation is also aligned with neglecting our emotional health. We have to address our underlying issues instead of spraying perfume (looking for a temporary fix) over the trash. Take the trash out!

> *There is a time for everything, and a season for every activity under heaven....A time to weep and a time to laugh, a time to mourn and a time to dance.* (Eccles. 3:1, 4)

~~Time Will Heal~~

I once came across an animated picture on Facebook of a clock trying to put a bandage on a wounded heart with stitches. I immediately thought the interpretation of this picture was "time will heal." However, it broke my heart to think that people actually believe this. What I envision for you is you handing your patched, stitched heart and your clock

---

[1] "Super Bug," interview by Van Jones, CNN, January 27, 2018.

to God. I also envision God extending His arms to reach for your heart and clock. Then He places them in the palm of His hand, only to peel away every bandage and the stitches holding your wound together, and shapes and molds your heart to His liking.

TIME DOESN'T HEAL

A mistake we often make is to say, "Time will heal," but in reality, time doesn't heal—God does. If you give your pain and cares to God, He will heal you in time. If you do not render your pain to God, it will begin to fester, take shape, and manifest in your relationships, workplace, decision-making, and all areas of your life.

Don't give time too much credit, because it doesn't have the authority to do the healing your heart is longing for. The only authority God gave time is to move forward, and while time is moving forward, you might think you have gotten over the trauma you've experience because you're not thinking about it. In reality, however, the pain you didn't resolve or face is still there, lingering in your mind.

Making Time

Yeah, yeah, yeah, I know you're thinking, *I have a busy schedule*. You are aware that you're in need of an emotional detox/ healing, but the pressure to keep up with life is weighing you down. You're always stressed out and feeling like you're about to drown. Perhaps you're a stay-at-home mom or dad, and your family demands so much of your time that you put your family's needs before yours; or maybe you work long hours and you barely have time to sleep. Whatever the circumstance, you keep putting off the desire to heal just so you can catch up with other things you're responsible for. At this point, you find yourself in survival mode.

So many people have been living like this their entire lives. It is imperative to make time to pray and seek emotional healing. You might have to squeeze in the time while your little ones nap or are at school, during your lunchtime at work, or before you go to bed. If you don't do this, you will find yourself feeling angry, and you might project that emotional baggage onto your friends, family, significant other, or colleagues.

We live in a time where we can get so distracted by our mobile devices and social media. We desire to hear God's voice and His instructions, but we're distracted. Maybe when you wake in the morning, before you pick up your phone to check what's new on social media or check your emails, take time to pray and write in that grief journal. This is a necessity for your well-being and for those who need you.

You deserve to be free from those emotional items of baggage!

Time of Reflection

- You are aware that you have an emotional scar.
- You have been placing Band-Aids over this scar.
- What are the Band-Aids?
- Are you putting expectations on how God should heal you?
- Are you afraid of being uncomfortable?
- Take the time to write in your grief journal.
- What's distracting you?

> *"For I know the plans I have for you,"* declares the Lord, *"plans to prosper you and not to harm you, plans to give you hope and a future."* (Jer. 29:11)

Jesus,

You are our Father. You want nothing but the best for us. At times, we have called on You for emotional healing, but we have put a limit on what You should do for us. Forgive us for putting a limit on Your hands and for turning to temporary fixes. We pray that You work on our hearts and that we trust the healing process You will put us through. Lord, teach us how to manage our time so we can speak to You and hear Your voice. Thank You for wanting to prosper us.

Feel free to say your own prayer. Release all your thoughts to Him. God is listening.

3

FACING TRUTH

GRIEF JOURNAL

When I was in college, my roommate at the time took a class called Spiritual Formation. One day, she came back to our room feeling uneasy. I asked her what was wrong, and she explained she had to write in a grief journal. I was a bit perplexed. I heard the word *journal* and instantly thought about the diaries/journal I had kept as a child, but the word *grief* went way over my head. All I could think was, *What's hard about writing in a journal?* Then she explained to me what a grief journal was and confided that she didn't want to deal with some emotional baggage she'd been carrying. I noticed her face expressed a lot of pain as she jotted down things from her past that had an effect on her life. I realized this journal was completely different from what I was used to.

YOU ARE NOT ALONE

SEEKING TRUTH

As you begin to write down the things that have been weighing you down, you may find yourself forced to face the truth. Truth is what we need; it's hard to face, yet once we begin to accept truth, liberation takes place. God wants His children to walk in His freedom; however, we are living in a world where truth is often photoshopped and freedom seems so farfetched. As you seek truth, there are lies that will linger in your mind; I would like to call these out, and I pray that you will allow God to chisel them away.

As you seek truth, you will have to embrace acceptance. Accept the things that happened in the past; accept the loss, and accept some changes. Sometimes we don't want to go through this journey because we believe the lie that we will have to go through it alone, but I want to remind you that you are not alone.

I wrote a letter inspired by scriptures I put together to affirm you. I pray these scriptures resonate with you.

My Beloved,

You are precious in my sight (Isa. 43:4). You have asked if I love you, and my answer is, yes, I have loved you with an everlasting love (Jer. 31:3). My love is so deep for you (Eph. 3:18). I am close to the broken-hearted (Ps. 34:18). Do not be dismayed, for I am your God. I will strengthen you and help you; I will uphold you with my righteous hand (Isa. 41:10). Whenever you feel unloved, unimportant, or insecure, remember to whom you belong (Eph. 2:19–22). You were created for a purpose (Rom. 9:17). You are forgiven (Ps. 103:12). I am the way, the truth, and the life (John 14:6). Cast all your cares on me and I will sustain you (Ps. 55:22). I will never leave you or forsake you (Exod. 14:14). Be strong. Be brave. Be fearless. You are never alone (Josh. 1:9).

Your heavenly Father

Phoropter

When my son turned four, I took him to his pediatrician for his annual checkup. First, his pediatrician assessed his emotional and social health. Then, she shifted her focus to his physical health and explained that he was of age to have his hearing and vision tested. After his examination, I was told that my son might need glasses. I was astonished. I am his mother; how could I have missed that? She gave me a referral to an optometrist. However, I was in denial. Maybe my son was just fooling around when he said he couldn't see the shapes and letters; maybe the optometrist would give me a different opinion.

A few weeks later, I took my son to the optometrist. The optometrist used an instrument called a phoropter. A phoropter has a series of lenses that the optometrist can adjust to varying degrees of power. After the optometrist placed the phoropter in front of my son's eyes, he instructed him to read the letters in front of him. As my son began to read the letters, the optometrist asked, "Can you see now?" When my son struggled to read the letters, the doctor refined the lenses' power.

All of a sudden, I heard my son exclaim, "Wow, I can see the letters better now!" The optometrist showed me an example of what my son's vision was like without the lens. It was a blur. I had to face the truth that my son needed glasses.

Writing in this grief journal may act as a phoropter for you. You may have experienced things that have caused you to be in denial. I challenge you, as God begins to adjust some things that you have failed to see, face the truth so you can be set free. Allow God to adjust your perspective.

Amazing Grace

"WAS BLIND, BUT NOW I SEE"

There are times in our lives when we do things we're not proud of. We sometimes try to justify the action or behavior, but in reality, we are the oppressor and not the victim. It's a hard pill to swallow to know that you're the oppressor. Failure to acknowledge it, however, does a great disservice to your growth. What do I mean by growth? I mean growing as in terms of being a better person, a person with integrity. Your ability to acknowledge you're at fault is a sign of maturity. However, justifying a bad action or behavior not only stunts growth, but it also covers the truth.

One person who stood out to me who admitted his actions were wrong was John Newton: "I hope it will always be a subject of humiliating reflection to me, that I was once an active instrument in a business at which my heart now shudders."[2] This was a public apology he made in a published pamphlet about slave trade.

---

[2] David B. Calhoun, "'Amazing Grace' John Newton and His Great Hymn," *Knowing & Doing*, Winter (November 22, 2013): |PAGE|)

While he was a slave trader, during a voyage home, he encountered a treacherous storm. Newton prayed to God and the ship miraculously drifted to safety. He then converted to Christianity, gradually changing his ways and eventually quitting the slaving profession. Decades later, he wrote "Amazing Grace," stating so eloquently, ". . . was blind but now I see." Newton had to face the truth that the slave trade was wrong; his actions caused Africans pain, which led him to quit that profession.

You are probably thinking, *Well, I haven't gone to the extent of John Newton.* My point is, ask yourself, *Have I played a role in hurting someone?* or *Am I currently causing someone pain?* If so, admit that you're wrong and face the truth so you can grow and allow the person you're hurting to grow as well.

Victim

GOD IS READY TO POUR GRACE AND REDEMPTION OVER YOU

Have you ever been a victim? Chances are, you have. There are various reasons why this is so. Perhaps you've been a victim of a heinous crime or some sort of abuse that had a psychological effect on you. We are all wired differently and have our own ways of coping with personal trauma. Some people choose to face what happened to them, and some choose not to deal with it at all. If you find yourself at a place where you haven't dealt with what happened to you, I pray that you dig deep and face the truth. Don't bury the reality with a temporary fix. God is ready to pour grace and redemption over you if you're willing to face the truth.

Victim Mentality

A victim mentality can be very comforting for someone who is not looking for growth. A person with a victim mentality blames their life challenges on others around them. The victim mentality can be debilitating. Due to the result of early life conditioning and coping mechanisms, a person may develop this mentality. People who suffer from a victim mentality generally engage in pity parties, exhibit anger, finger-point, and constantly blame other people or situations for their misery. They also keep reliving past painful memories that make them feel like a victim. Additionally, people with a victim mentality generally feel powerless in their circumstances. They also become very defensive when given constructive criticism.

Do you think you have a victim mentality? It takes someone looking for a breakthrough to admit and face the truth that they are clinging to a victim mentality. If you find yourself at this place, you're hindering yourself from experiencing growth and the joy of the Lord. Nehemiah 8:10 says, "Don't be dejected and sad, for the Joy of the Lord is your strength." It is time to explore where you have acquired this victim mentality and break free from it. You are not a victim—you are victorious. See yourself as a survivor and take control over your thoughts. You are a conqueror, but this statement is true only if you seek God's strength and not sympathy from others.

Remember, this chapter is called "Facing Truth." If you feel that this discussion of victim mentality has stirred you the wrong way (you feel upset), please take a moment to explore what you are feeling and then take responsibility for that attitude.

> *My grace is sufficient for you, for my power is made perfect in weakness.* (2 Cor. 12:19)

TIME OF REFLECTION

- Understand what a grief journal is.
- Seek truth from the oppressor's point of view and the victim's perspective.

- Are you an oppressor, or are you a victim?
- Admit your wrongdoing.
- Accept and face the truth.
- Do you have a victim mentality?
- Break free from the victim mentality!

Heavenly Father,

You know our hearts. You've seen what we have gone through. I ask that You teach us how to face truth and not bury it when problems arise. God, I ask You to rest upon our hearts, teach us Your ways, and let us put our trust in You. We thank You for redemption and for Your grace that has carried us through.

Feel free to say your own prayer.

4

THE BIG F-WORD

Forgiveness

Forgiveness is a word that some people can't comprehend when someone has done them wrong. However, forgiveness produces freedom, peace of mind, joy, and growth. Forgiveness is the key to emotional healing. It's a choice that you have to make, yet it's the hardest decision to make.

Did you know forgiveness is good for your health? It can relieve stress and lower blood pressure. According to Karen Swartz, M.D., chronic anger can increase heart rate, blood pressure, and blood glucose. This is known as the fight-or-flight syndrome. When these physical changes occur, the risk of depression, heart disease, diabetes, and other conditions increases.[3]

How can you successfully forgive? When you make the decision to forgive, it is more than just saying the words—it's an active process. It does not happen with the snap of your fingers. You really have to make a conscious decision to forgive deeply. Forgiveness may require you to reflect so you can have empathy for that person's behavior or actions. Whether the person deserves it or not, you're setting your heart free when you forgive.

FORGIVING SOMEONE BREAKS THE CYCLE AND THE RISK OF YOU HURTING SOMEONE ELSE

In 2015, Dr. Sombat Jitmoud's son was murdered while delivering pizza. During the court hearing in 2017, Dr. Jitmoud forgave the man who pleaded guilty to his son's murder. In an interview, Dr. Jitmoud said something so profound to the man who killed his son. He said, "I blame the devil who misguided you and misled you to do such a horrible

---

3   Temma Ehrenfeld, "Forgiveness Is Good for You," *Psychology Today,* November 3, 2016, |PAGE|, https://www.psychologytoday.com/us/blog/open-gently/201611/forgiving-is-good-you).

crime."[4] Dr. Jitmoud had empathy for the person who had done him wrong. He set his heart and mind free and also released the young man from his guilt.

My therapist once told me, "Hurt people hurt people." Forgiving someone breaks the cycle and the risk of you hurting someone else. When you hang on to grudges, you are more likely to experience severe depression and post-traumatic stress disorder.[5]

It is often easy to forgive someone who has apologized or shown remorse, but what about the person who isn't sorry for what they've done to you? We often look for closure by expecting that person to apologize, but how about we take the initiative to create our own closure?

When you don't forgive, you give that person power to fuel your anger and resentment. You're allowing the person to have dominion over your heart and mind, keeping you imprisoned. Don't wait for someone to be remorseful or apologize to you before you forgive; you might end up waiting awhile

Father God, that i was it is only By your grace dear able to forgive thank You

[4] Marwa Eltagouri, "Acts of Faith," *Washington Post*, November 17, 2017, |PAGE|, https://www.washingtonpost.com/news/acts-of-faith/wp/2017/11/10/why-this-father-hugged-the-man-who-helped-kill-his-son/).

[5] Temma Ehrenfeld, "Forgiveness Is Good for You," *Psychology Today*, November 3, 2016, |PAGE|, https://www.psychologytoday.com/us/blog/open-gently/201611/forgiving-is-good-you)

because they might not be sorry! This can lead to disappointment, so let go of that expectation.

Also, keep in mind that an apology may not change your relationship with that person. Forgiveness doesn't always need reconciliation. For example, if a woman was in an abusive relationship and summons the courage to leave this man, it wouldn't be a wise decision for her to reconcile the relationship, lest she find herself bound in an abusive situation again. Therefore, she can forgive her abuser, but trying to salvage the relationship may not work to her advantage.

Forgive Yourself

Forgiveness includes forgiving yourself. You may be holding on to guilt and shame. When someone's morals and values have evolved, they might feel guilt or shame for an action that was done to them or an action they did. Nevertheless, there must come a point where you make room to accept what happened. Accept that the past is the past. Focus on what you can learn from it instead of what you can undo. Let go of what you've done or the things you have absolutely no control over.

Release any bitterness to God. Express your heart to Him. As you begin to write in your grief journal, record your biggest regrets. You can start with saying, "Father, I regret . . ." or "Father, I'm hurt because . . ." There's nothing He can't do. Allow God's love to set you free. Jesus died for you and me to be set free. Ask God for a better understanding of His love for you.

Our Father wants to forgive us, but if we don't forgive others and ourselves, He won't. Your main goal is to release your regrets instead of keeping them stored in your mind. Remember the analogy of the sink flooding in chapter 1. Well, an unforgiving heart can clog your sink.

> *For if you forgive others their trespasses, your heavenly Father will also...*
> (Matt. 6:14)

Repent

According to Merriam-Webster's dictionary, *repent* means "to turn from sin and dedicate oneself to the amendments of one's life."[6] No one on this earth is perfect; we all have sinned or hurt someone. Forgiveness and repentance work hand in hand. When someone repents, it allows God to forgive them.

---

[6] *Merriam-Webster,* s.v. "repent," definition 1, https://www.merriam-webster.com/dictionary/repent).

Letting go of the things from your past sometimes will require you to repent. Repent from anger, guilt, shame, lies, hate, malice—all the things that have been holding your mind hostage. There comes a point where you have to reach a place of humility and confess and repent to God. Repentance requires you to change your mindset and habits. It is never too late to repent; please make the time to do so. Emotional healing doesn't happen overnight; it's a process. Repentance can help with the process of the emotional healing your heart is longing for.

> *Now repent of your sins and turn to God, so that your sins may be wiped away.* (Acts 3:19 NLT)

TIME OF REFLECTION

- Learn how to be more forgiving.
- Do you have someone you need to forgive today? Let go of the grudges. Forgive because your life is depending on it.
- Forgive yourself and let go.
- Repent and let God have His way.

> *This, then, is how you should pray: "Our Father in heaven, hallowed be your name, your kingdom come, your will be*

done, on earth as it is in heaven. Give us today our daily bread. And forgive us our debts as we also have forgiven our debtors. And lead us not into temptation, but deliver us from the evil one." (Matt. 6:9–13)

Dear God,

Help Your beloved let go of the people who have hurt them. Set their hearts free and teach Your beloved to forgive as You have forgiven. I pray that You create a clean heart and renew a right spirit within them. Show them how to forgive themselves and surrender their circumstances to You. Thank You for the gift of repentance and forgiveness.

Feel free to say what's on your heart.

5

WHEN LIFE HITS YOU

We are all candidates for facing life's adversities; the worst thing, however, is when it hits you unexpectedly and completely blindsides you. I live in New York, and in the winter, we normally have blizzards. Whenever a blizzard is coming, the supermarkets are packed with people frantically shopping for the essentials before the storm hits. Everybody gets prepared for the storm. There is little peace even when people know they have had time to prepare for the blizzard.

THE STORM IS COMING

One spring season, the weather fluctuated between sixty and ninety degrees. On one particular day, the meteorologist said that it was going to be eighty-five degrees and humid, and later that day, a storm was expected. I was at the park with my daughter, and the sun was beaming; the heat almost felt oppressive. We took water breaks to stay hydrated. I waited for a friend while I chased my daughter around the park. When my friend arrived, we walked around the park, and I couldn't believe a storm was coming. The sun was still shining, and not one dark cloud was in sight. We continued to walk for a while and then decided to find a bench to sit on. Within a matter of minutes of our making that decision, the bright sun vanished and the dark clouds began to roll in. I said to my friend, "The storm is coming. Let's leave the park."

Here came the storm the meteorologist had warned us about. As we left the park, the wind picked up and the clouds darkened. We quickened our pace, trying to beat the rain. We found shelter just in time and stepped into a nearby diner as the rain began.

As I sat in the diner, I thought to myself, *Wow, if only we had the chance to know when a storm was coming to wreck our lives.* Unfortunately, we don't always get the forecast for the storms life will bring our way. It doesn't matter how great of a person you are, how strong your relationship is with God, or even the number of good deeds you have done—life's storms will come to you. You can't escape them. You may suffer the loss of a loved one, a grim diagnosis, a painful breakup, or some other storm of life; all these factors can put so much stress on your heart.

WE ARE NOT EXEMPT FROM HIS GRACE

Storms can rob us of our strength and hope and leave us with only an ounce of faith. When asked the infamous question "How are you doing?" we tend to mask the circumstances of our storm with the response "I'm fine." Either we don't want to be a burden to people, or we don't trust them enough to share our personal lives with them. Instead, we suppress all the emotions stirring inside in an effort to show that we are fine or tough, and we mask our pain with a smile.

I want you to know, however, that although you are not exempt from adversity, you are also not exempt from His grace. God's grace is sufficient for you, as Scripture says: "But he said to me, 'My grace is sufficient for you, my power is made perfect in weakness'" (2 Cor. 12:9). God's grace will carry you through the worst storms that life can bring. However, if you suppress your emotions, how can you feel and embrace God's grace? It's okay not to be okay; it's okay to feel.

Fight

Do you know someone who is afraid to get into a physical altercation when they feel like their life is being threatened? I have a sibling who has always said, "I'm not a fighter. I can't fight to save my life." Every time my sister made this statement, I laughed at her. Even though my sister is three years older than me, when we were growing up, I had to be ready to protect her if someone tried to get into a physical altercation with her.

Although my sister fears getting into a physical fight to defend herself, she still has a battle to fight, like all of us. Maybe you're fighting an illness, fighting to keep your marriage, fighting to make ends meet, fighting to have joy, and, over all, fighting not to lose your mind. None of us can escape this fight. We all have something we're fighting for or fighting with, and this can be emotionally draining.

Writing in a grief journal is a form of fighting. As you write, you will experience emotions that you will either fight to release or fight to suppress. I encourage you to keep fighting, calling on the Spirit of the Lord, regardless of the circumstances you may be facing. "'Not by might nor by power, but by my Spirit,' says the Lord" (Zech. 4:6). Fight for your joy, peace of mind, and emotional healing!

You Are Not Alone

Sometimes when we are going through something difficult, we feel consumed with guilt, shame, or despair. In our turmoil, we feel alone, but that's a lie. The devil likes to prey on people who feel emotionally wrecked. He likes to feed lies that will develop into emotions that can keep them bound. The devil wants you to think you can't get healed; he wants you to keep those negative thoughts in your mind and stay addicted to whatever substance you've picked.

The truth, however, is Jesus has already set you free and paid the price on Calvary. Nevertheless, you might be thinking, *How am I free when I feel like this? I struggle with* _____ (insert whatever you struggle with). The devil is a thief who comes only to steal, kill, and destroy your purpose. He wants to isolate you and make you feel like there's no hope and no one will understand you. That's a lie!

YOU HAVE TO FIGHT THE URGE TO ISO-LATE YOURSELF

The devil wants to keep you in the dark so you can't see the promises of God. When you start your grief journal, know that God is and will always be there, ready to heal your broken heart and bind up your wounds (Ps. 147:3). You have to fight the urge to isolate yourself when you're struggling with guilt, shame, or despair. It's okay to want time to be alone, but seek alone time with God where you can be filled with His truth. When the negative thoughts begin, speak against them. Don't let them lure you into a quiet room, or your bed, where they can tie up your mind and keep you hostage.

You are not alone, you are not alone, you are not alone! I wrote this three times to emphasize that whatever you're going through, don't believe the lie that you're alone. God is with you!

Overcoming Depression

I gave my life to Christ when I was ten years old. In the years before, I had already struggled with feeling insignificant, but something sparked inside me at the age of ten. To those who knew me, they saw a happy, silly, energetic child, but deep down inside, I wasn't happy. At that young age, I had already mastered putting a mask on my face and saying "I'm fine" when asked how I was doing. When people were around, I always tried to be funny and make people laugh. However, when I was home and alone, I would sit in the dark and hear, *Nobody loves you, You're stupid,* or *You're ugly.* Sadly, certain people around me actually ignited those thoughts I heard in the dark.

Though people always surrounded me, I felt lonely and hopeless. I wondered, *How can I feel like this when I gave my life to Christ?* As a ten-year-old, I couldn't make sense of what was going on. I had a continual urge to isolate myself, and I spent many years crying myself to sleep. As I grew older, suicidal thoughts began tormenting me. Whenever I heard someone had passed away, I would be jealous because it wasn't me. I spent seven birthdays angry because I had reached another year. To those reading this, you might think I was ungrateful for life, but I simply couldn't understand what was going on and to whom I should speak.

When I was seventeen, I realized I was battling with depression. One night, I spoke to my sister about how I felt, and she prayed with me. God delivered me from depression that night, but the entire healing process was a long journey.

I started spending more time with God, and I began to journal. At the time, I didn't write to heal (grief journal), but merely recorded what I heard the Lord speaking to me. When negative thoughts came, I knew not to isolate myself, because that was a trap. I learned the difference between isolating myself to be in the presence of God and isolating myself to be in the presence of negative thoughts. I prayed more, read the Bible more, and learned not to let myself slip away with negative thoughts.

After I was delivered from depression at the age of seventeen, I experienced two incidents that took a toll on me, but there was a difference this time—I had hope. I was a new person, and I knew I had to verbalize the thoughts that would try to pull me away. I now knew that when facing a difficult circumstance, I had to pray even harder and fight back. Writing in a grief journal and praying helped me face depression from a different angle. However, as I learned, grief journaling is not a one-time exercise. "It is best done as a regular spiritual discipline," says Dr. Ron Walborn.[7] I learned to grieve and allow God to do the healing that I needed.

If you are struggling with depression, it is okay to seek professional help. There is nothing wrong with doing that.

It's Okay to Cry

When someone is experiencing pain, or even joy, they may shed a tear. Many times, however, people shy away from crying because they're worried about

---

[7] Ron Walborn, Dr., "It's Ok to Cry," *The Alliance*, September 16, 2016, |PAGE|, https://www.cmalliance.org/alife/its-ok-to-cry/).

what others may think of them. But God gave us emotions, and it's okay to express them in a healthy way. Even Jesus, who is the Son of God, *wept* because of the death of his friend Lazarus (John 11:35).

According to psychologists, crying benefits your health[8] and is actually good for you. It is a sign of resilience and strength, and it is also a great way to relieve stress and filter out worry and grief. Emotional tears release hormones that escape from your body, improving your mood. On the other hand, holding back your tears can cause long-term psychological damage. Bottling up your emotions can lead to depression, anxiety, and drug abuse.

The way you cry can't be controlled. It's a genuine expression of your emotions. With that being said, don't be afraid to cry; let it out to your heavenly Father. Allow the Holy Spirit to comfort you. He wants nothing but the best for you. God longs for His children to live in peace, not in pieces. Jeremiah 29:11 says, "'For I know the plans I have for you,' declares the Lord, ‹plans to prosper you and not to harm you, plans to give you hope and a future.'" If you're clinging to or suppressing things from your past, you cannot fully receive God's plans for your life.

---

[8] Ashley Marcin, "9 Ways Crying May Benefit Your Health," *HealthLine*, September 14, 2017, |PAGE|.

In-To-Me-See (Intimacy)

The best part of all this is that it will lead you to find a sweet spot with God; in other words, a place of intimacy with our Father. Despite all the hurt and betrayal, intimacy with God will break down the defensive walls you have built. Sometimes God will let emotions you've suppressed resurface. He brings out these emotions to get your attention so you can bring them to Him. When you bring all your pain and worries to God, you allow Him to see your heart. He then can exchange your pain for peace and healing.

The heart is where we store our secrets; it is the place of intimacy. According to the dictionary, *intimacy* is defined as "showing a close union."[9] Psalm 139:23 says, "Search me, oh God, and know my heart: try me and know my thoughts." Intimacy allows God to search your heart, look into you (in-to-me-see), and reveal things that may be weighing you down. In this book, I have written prayers and shared scriptures that will aid you in the process of detoxing your mind. I pray the wall you have built tumbles down so that God may have full access to you.

---

[9] *Merriam-Webster Dictionary,* s.v., "intimacy," https://www. merriam-webster.com/dictionary/intimacy).

Front-Row Seat

Whenever people are planning to attend a show, a sporting event, or a concert, they are often willing to pay more or arrive early to reserve the best seat at the venue. People usually want the front-row seat or something as close to the front as possible because it makes them feel like they're part of the show. However, when it comes to something like comedy club, school, or church, people may shy away from the front-row seat because it renders them vulnerable. In class, you can't sneak in a nap or eat a snack discreetly in the front-row seat.

When life hits you and you're feeling discouraged, see it as God putting you in the front-row seat to experience His love and grace. You get to experience the God who heals, provides, and showers you with all the other great qualities He possesses. Front-row seats may come at a cost, but when God is in it, you'll experience His unfailing love.

Trust the Process

As you begin to reveal to God what is on your heart, you will certainly go through a process of healing and restoration. Oftentimes, on a journey like this, people will tell you to "trust the process." I say don't trust the process, but trust the one (God) who is putting you through the process. If you trust the process, it will shift your focus and you might become disappointed. Trusting the process instead of God is like putting your GPS on silent; that will make you rely on yourself to look at the GPS instead of listening to the voice for direction. If you put your GPS on silent, you will have to take your eyes off the road to see where to make the next turn or head for the next exit, and taking your eyes off the road can lead to an accident.

Gracious Father,

I thank You for Your love, mercy, and compassion toward all of us. I acknowledge Your greatness. It is a privilege for us to come to You and give our fears, pain, worries, and burdens to You in exchange for peace.

Comforter, I pray for Your beloved, who chose to earnestly seek You. I pray for their emotional healing; heal their hearts and help them forgive those who have hurt them in the past. Set their hearts free so they can live their lives to their fullest potential. Father, as they embark on this journey, show them what's cluttering their mind. Let it be so clear to them the need to let go of those things so they can be receptive to all the good things You have in store for them.

Holy Spirit, manifest in their lives. May Your beloved continuously feel Your presence as they began to release things that have been holding them down and hindering them from seeing the love You have for them. Saturate Your beloved's heart until there's no room for the pain from sexual abuse, physical abuse, verbal abuse, divorce, loss, abandonment, insignificance, betrayal, and any other thing they may be struggling with. I speak the fruit of the Spirit over their lives: "But the fruit of the Spirit is love, joy, peace, forbearance, kindness, goodness, faithfulness" (Gal. 5:22).

I thank You, Comforter, for Your love. It is an honor to know that You would leave Your throne to comfort us when we need it the most. May this journaling experience draw us nearer to the cross and open the eyes of our hearts to receive Your goodness.

> *Taste and see that the LORD is good; blessed is the one who takes refuge in Him.* (Ps. 34:8)

TIME OF REFLECTION

- How are you really doing? Before you answer that question, really take the time to examine how you are doing.
- Crying is healthy.
- Experience God's grace from the front-row seat.

Feel free to pray and say what's on your heart.

WRITE TO HEAL

Why Is This Journaling Exercise Important?

This journaling experience allows you to see where habits and certain behaviors stem from, thus enabling you to learn more about your own psychology. It helps you access and assess situations and circumstances that may have tainted your view of the life God has in store for you. You may have experienced a divorce, rejection from someone you gave your heart to, the loss of a job or loved one, a violation of trust, a diagnosis of illness, or chronic illness; all these circumstances can leave you grief-stricken.

You never know what someone went through or is going through. I once had a colleague who was a very sweet woman; she was always smiling and sharing a joke. Her smile was contagious, and all her students loved her. She was a wonderful person. One day, during our lunch break, we were talking about our families. She decided to share her story with me about the several miscarriages she had suffered before she gave birth to her son. I was amazed that she was still smiling despite all the miscarriages.

I asked her how she had dealt with her loss, and her response was, "I wrote a letter to one of the babies that I lost." Fast forward to five years since she shared her story with me. She came to mind as I was writing this book, so I reached out to her to share a little of her experience with writing to heal. This is what she said:

> *My way of handling it was by crying all the time, being angry at God for making me lose the baby, and basically isolating myself. After writing the letter, it somehow gave me inner peace because I felt so close to the baby, like the baby was with me. Also, while writing, I somehow felt joy, and I wasn't as angry.*
>
> *I did not start out writing with the intention to heal, but I found out later*

that it did help me with healing. It was important for me to write because I felt guilty that I lost the baby, and I had to let the baby know how sorry I was that I couldn't save him, and that he should know all the plans I had for him. Now that I felt better, I did pray and ask God to forgive me for being angry with Him, because He knows better.

Mary's story was so powerful to me. I am so glad that in spite of her loss, she found inner peace and joy. Your story may not be similar or even close to Mary's; however, I am praying for your inner peace and joy. As I said earlier, God wants His children in live in peace, not pieces.

My sophomore year at Nyack College was an emotional year for me. I experienced betrayal, and a friend passed away. I had trouble processing all the things life was throwing at me. I sought counseling with my campus pastor, Pastor Kelvin. In one of my counseling sessions, he mentioned an assignment Ron Walborn gave the students in his Spiritual Formation class. It was the same assignment that my freshman roommate had been given, which was to write in a grief journal, and that's what Pastor Kelvin suggested I do. When Pastor Kelvin made his suggestion, he had a vision of me lying on a hammock, telling God my pain.

I was a bit apprehensive at first and tried to avoid it, but I knew it was imperative for me to write. God was tugging at me to release what was on my heart. There were days that I felt emotionally uncomfortable, and I knew that was a reminder that I needed to write to heal. As I mentioned before, the grief journal is where I made the connection on why I had always believed I was slow, and was able to identify many other toxic emotions that had kept me bound.

I REALIZED HOW IMPORTANT IT IS TO GRIEVE NOT ONLY PEOPLE YOU MAY HAVE LOST, BUT MISSED OPPORTUNITIES

Charlie Mackington is a former student of Ron Walborn. When he took his class, like the other students, he was required to write in a grief journal. This is what Charlie said:

> *Dr. Ron Walborn asked us to write grief journals, and while I understood the assignment on a surface level, it didn't do much for me at that time because there were things I was not ready to deal with. This morning, however, I*

realized how important it is to grieve not only people you may have lost, but missed opportunities, things that happen to you, or things that happen because of you. It's important to grieve those seasons in your life. We are all carrying baggage, whether we admit it or not. There are some things that have happened to us that we may not realize have hurt us, or we don't acknowledge that they hurt us.

Grieving comes before healing. Grieving is not one specific emotion, but rather conflicting feelings caused by the end of or a change in a familiar pattern of behavior. Take time to do a self-evaluation. What are the things you are not healed from? What are the things that trigger you? There may be some things that you aren't yet able to grieve because the pain is still too real, but immediately take stock of those things also. Pain is a part of life, but healing is also part of life. Pain. Grieve. Heal.

With this journaling experience, you will be able to pull out the weeds that are depriving your garden of growth. Once I became aware of how much this word (slow) affected me, I realized it was simply a weed in my garden that I had to allow God to pull out by the root. It was prohibiting me from living a productive life.

I did a little research about weeding a garden and learned the benefits. While weeding a garden is interesting in itself, it also serves as an example that offers you a way to reflect on your own life journey.

Why You Need to Weed Your Garden

1. **Weeds compete with crops.**

   A plant needs sun, rain, and the soil's nutrients to grow. The fewer the weeds in your garden, the more your vegetables will grow. When you're applying this to your own life, remember that you need the Son of God (Jesus) and the fruit of the Spirit (love, joy, peace, patience, kindness, goodness, faithfulness, gentleness, self-control [Gal. 5:22]).

   We all will experience grief and what we call the storms of life. What do storms bring? You got it—rain! God allows storms to come so that you can grow. However, if you allow anger, bitterness, and other negative emotions to permeate your heart and mind, they will compete with the development of the fruit of the Spirit.

Lastly, the Word of God works as the soil's nutrients that we need in order to grow.

2. **Weeds block out sunlight and steal water.**

Weeds grow aggressively and begin to block out the sun. Let's talk about the weed of fear. It magnifies lies in our minds and blocks out what God thinks of us and has for us. John 7:37 says, "If anyone is thirsty, let him come to Me and drink." Jesus is the living water we need to thrive in life. Don't let fear block out the Son of God and steal the flow of His living water.

3. **Weeds crowd out space.**

Each plant in a garden has its own root zone. When the root zone of one plant invades the space of another plant, that plant becomes stressed. Weeds share space not only above soil, but below it as well.

When I think about how each plant has its own root zone, I am reminded that God has a purpose for everyone. As Exodus 9:16 says, "But for this purpose I have raised you up, to show you my power, so that my name may be proclaimed in all the earth." He places us in a zone where we can grow and fulfill our purpose. When we're not emotionally healthy, our purpose is invaded. When we don't know our purpose, stress often results.

Last but not least, this journaling experience is important because it allows you to feel. My dear friend Priscilla once said, "We are told that if you're hurt, don't cry—move on. If a child falls, we tell them to get up and not to cry. We have been taught to suck it up and move on. Are we not allowed to feel anymore?" When we face adversity, we sometimes tend to rush the process (healing and grieving).

Time of Reflection

- What are the weeds in your garden that need to be pulled up?
- How are they affecting your life?
- How long have they been growing in your garden?

Words have the power to heal you or hurt you. You have the authority to take a stance and declare great things in your life. Here is a declaration for you to speak over your life:

I (insert name) have weeds in my garden that I need to pull up by the root. I will no longer let them affect me or control my life. I will not lean on my understanding. I will seek God and allow Him to work in me. I am not the person I used to be. God is doing a new thing in me, and I will trust Him. I am His child, and He loves me. I can do anything with Christ who gives me strength; therefore, I will not be afraid to kill the weeds that are in my life.

Feel free to say your own declaration.

7

WHERE DO I BEGIN?

You've read testimonials, I've shared some of my life experiences with you, and you've had times of reflection. Are you wondering how to start this grief journal? You are free to type on your computer or write on the pages provided in this book. The best part is you don't have to worry about punctuation or grammatical errors. This experience is for you and God. He does not care if it's legible. He wants authenticity!

Focus on searching for the meaning of challenging experiences you've dealt with in your life. You may not find the answers to questions like, "Why did this person have to die?" or "Why didn't this relationship last?" but you will be able to vent your fears, frustration, worries, and pain to God. You don't have to be a great writer to get your healing through writing.

In 2016, Ron Walborn wrote a blog, "It's Ok to Cry."[10] In one part of the blog, he shared how to start a grieving exercise:

> Begin a bullet list of your losses. Start whereever the most pain arises. It doesn't have to be chronological. Fix your eyes on Jesus (Heb. 12:2) and say, "Search me, O God, and know my heart; test me and know my anxious thoughts. See if there is any offensive way in me, and lead me in the way everlasting" (Ps. 139:23–24). Ask the Lord, "Where do you want me to go first?" Allow the Lord to bring the incident or memory to mind of when the loss happened. Write out the memory and engage with it emotionally. Do not censor your words....Don't stop when it starts to get uncomfortable or painful. That is a sign you are getting right to the place that you need to

---

[10] Ron Walborn, Dr., "It's Ok to Cry," *The Alliance*, September 16, 2016, |PAGE|, https://www.cmalliance.org/alife/its-ok-to-cry/).

feel and release....Find a safe person
to help you process this pain.

HE WASN'T ABSENT IN MY TIME OF GRIEF

Go at Your Pace

In November 2015, my husband and I experienced a miscarriage. We were devastated; it was a harsh reality I did not want to face. I cried when we went to the emergency room, and I thought that provided enough time to cry and move on. After the trip to the emergency room, I planned to go to work the next day, but my husband suggested that I stay home. At first, I was reluctant to heed his suggestion, but deep down inside, I knew it was something I needed. I ended up taking a whole week off. I cried and cried some more, and my husband and I expressed how we felt. We allowed this loss to draw us closer. When I couldn't find words to say, I called on the name of Jesus. I knew He wasn't absent in my time of grief, so I laid my pain at the cross. I'm not saying it only took a week for me to grieve over the miscarriage; however, I was able to release the pain of loss instead of sweeping my emotions under the rug. Every now and then, I still think about our little angel, but I have found solace, knowing that I will one day meet our baby.

> *The Lord is close to the brokenhearted and saves those who are crushed in spirit.* (Ps. 34:18)

During the week I took off, my coworker kept calling me, in hopes that I would return to work sooner because the office was getting very busy. Through that experience, I learned some things. First, some people don't have the proper sympathy etiquette. As a result, their choice of words can wreak harm in times of grief. Some words or actions can make you feel pressured to rush through your time of grieving, and other words make you feel guilty for even crying. Some people will even compare your experience to theirs to make you feel what you're feeling isn't that bad. When I experienced a miscarriage, I was six weeks pregnant. I heard people say "well, you weren't that far along... I had miscarriage I was much further along." Hearing those words made feel like I didn't have a reason to be sad, I should get over this loss faster. Those conversations didn't make me feel any better it just made me feel like I didn't have have a reason to cry.

To the person who's been grieving over a love one's death and it has been over five years, it is ok, grief has no expiration date. To the person whose circumstances has been down-played. I'm sorry. Your feelings a real and indeed valid. You might get the notion that you should move on at a certain pace, that may lead you to suppress your pain in order to function in the real world. You are allowed to feel and still survive.

Second, it's okay to lament, to cry. In chapter 5, I explained why it is okay to cry and the health benefits that come from it. Don't let anyone rush you or deprive you from the healing you you deserve. It's your heart, not theirs be free from allowing people dictate how long you should grieve. Invite Jesus into your grieving journey, and allow Him to heal you and help you grow.

> *I am the vine: you are the branches. If you remain in me and I in you, you will bear much fruit, apart from me you can do nothing.* (John 15:5)

Self-Care

Whenever I scroll through social media, I see almost everyone talking about self-care. Self-care is taking the time to pursue some of the activities that nurture you. It is for you and provided by you. You might see someone post a picture of themselves exercising, drinking a glass of wine, or even going on a vacation. Somehow, these people have identified their own needs and taken the initiative to provide care for themselves. Taking the initiative to take proper care of yourself is imperative.

Parents and guardians, this is for you. As a parent, you inevitably put your children's needs before your own. In reality, however, you need self-care moments because it is beneficial for your mental health. It is extremely difficult to be the best parent you're intended to be if you don't practice self-care. You might even find yourself projecting your emotions onto your children if you don't take time for your mental health. Writing a grief journal is a form of self-care that will benefit not only you, but also your children.

Time of Reflection

- Take a moment to think about what you're going to write in your grief journal.
- Have you ever felt pressured to move on?
- Be selfish to be selfless.

Gracious Redeemer,

You know me more than I know myself; show me the specific area in my life that I need to work on. My busy life and my surroundings are pressuring me to move on and not deal with what's weighing me down. Teach me how to be attentive to my spiritual needs before I consume my spirit with the pressures of the world.

Thank You for listening and being there for me.

Feel free to share your own prayer.

8

Lost in Loss

Types of Loss

Loss is something we can't prevent. Sometimes it comes without warning, and other times, if we're fortunate, we have a chance to prepare for it. Loss can change the course of your life as it brings up feelings and memories. When you hear the word *loss*, death likely comes to mind; however, there are different types of loss that are not limited to death, such as loss of freedom, loss of innocence, loss of a job, loss of body function, loss of home or property, loss of identity, and many more. All these types of losses can make you feel lost and leave you in distress.

She Loss Her Childhood

Ihave a dear friend who is the eldest of four. She was raised in an unreasonably strict household. She didn't have the best relationship with her mother. At a young age, she had to step up and take responsibility for her siblings, thus depriving her of many common childhood experiences, such as learning how to ride a bike or skate. When she was in elementary school, she was molested by a much older man. She kept this a secret because she didn't know how to express what was happening to her. The only places she was allowed to go were school and church. She spent most of her life raising her siblings.

My friend expressed to me that she lost sight of her childhood by blocking out the sexual abuse, and she learned to suppress the emotions from the physical, verbal, and emotional abuse she endured from her mother. As an adult, she still gets angry and feels hurt when she thinks about what she endured as a child. The loss of her childhood has affected her adulthood in the sense that she has had unhealthy relationships as she searched for love and the sense of a loving embrace.

This woman has not fully dealt with the loss of her childhood, though she is aware of the strength and wisdom she has gained through her life experiences. Over the years, she has reflected and realized that many of her pitfalls stem from the loss of her childhood. Like my dear friend, many of us have endured a loss that we can't seem to get over, but it is important that we fully deal with our losses so they won't affect our future.

WE DEAL WITH LOSS DIFFERENTLY

Write About Your Loss

Experiencing loss can put us in a dark place. Some people never recover after a loss because they don't know how to process it. We are all different and deal with loss differently. Some people find ways to unleash their grief, while some don't grieve at all because they fear that once they give in to grief, they won't be able to stop. Some people that I've encouraged to grieve have responded with "I'm afraid to grieve because the pain is overwhelming," or "What if I grieve and can't stop?" or

"Grieving won't bring back what I loss."

Although it is true that grieving does not bring back your loss, it is nonetheless necessary. Writing down your feelings and experiences can help you process grief. Refusing to grieve prohibits you from experiencing joy and stunts your growth. If you have a fear of grieving because you're afraid you might get stuck there, include God in your time of grieving.

He will guide you if you allow Him to. Some people, however, when they experience loss, blame God; they therefore resent Him and exclude Him out of a journey He wants to be part of.

Time of Reflection

- Which loss have you experienced?
- Are you afraid to grieve?
- Include God in your process of grieving.
- Write about your experience with loss.

Blessed are those who mourn, for they will be comforted. (Matt. 5:4)

Dear God,
I have experienced a loss that has broken me. Help me understand that You are in control; You're here to comfort and heal me. Teach me how to get through the season instead of asking to get over it. I give You my broken heart and hurting soul. I trust that You will mend my broken heart. Thank You for loving me and comforting me.

Feel free to say your own prayer.

9

UNDERSTANDING GRIEF

There are five stages of grief, but not everyone goes through all of them or goes through them in a specific order, since we are all wired differently.

Grief is a response to loss. At first, I was a little apprehensive to talk about understanding grief because I was thinking, *What does the loss of a loved one or something have to do with detoxing your mind?* Then the Holy Spirit made it clear to me that some people haven't gotten over the death of a loved one or a loss in general. They have developed bad habits, building a wall of defense around their heart and assuming blame for the loss. They are stuck in the anger stage of grief. Negative thoughts have begun to fester in their hearts and they can't move forward.

It is important to talk about the five stages of grief: (1) denial, (2) anger, (3) bargaining, (4) depression, and (5) acceptance. Sometimes we don't comprehend our response to loss and try to ease our grief with things that won't help in the process.

Shock/Denial

In chapter 5, I spoke on unexpected tragedies that come into our lives. In those cases, shock is often the first reaction. For instance, if someone receives a phone call about their loved one having passed away, they will, of course, be shocked and in total disbelief. In this stage, the news makes no sense; many people feel numb because they cannot comprehend the impact of the loss. Denying the reality may work to refrain us from feeling the pain while the state of shock lingers. Shock and denial work in conjunction with each other. They help protect us from feeling pain's intensity.

Denial serves a normal purpose. It is a way for the mind to protect us from feeling more pain. Eventually, however, denial begins to diminish as we begin to face the truth. Some people are not able to acknowledge their loss, so they find ways to numb their pain, such as using drugs. God does not want you to be stuck in denial. If you refuse to feel the pain, you are depriving yourself from receiving the love, joy, and peace He has for you.

Bargaining

Bargaining may occur prior to a loved one's death, or it may happen after the loved one has passed. It is a phase in the grief process. In this stage, a person may ask God to spare a loved one's life by offering a change of behavior or commitment: *I will pray more*, or *I will read my Bible more*. It is common for people to bargain, but at a certain point, they have to face reality and begin the healing process.

Anger

On September 22, 2016, I was pregnant with my daughter. I remember that day so clearly. I woke up to feeling my daughter's kicks and counting down the days until I gave birth. My joy instantly was ripped from me when I received a phone call from my brother. He asked me, "Have you heard about Christina?"

My response was, "No, did she get discharged?" My friend had been in the hospital for a couple of days at the time.

My brother paused before uttering the next few words that would pierce my heart. "She...she has gone home. The Lord has called her home."

My knees buckled, and I began to weep uncontrollably. I couldn't even hold the phone, and I lost my balance. I didn't hear anything else. My husband had to get me in the bed. I was in shock, saying, "No, she can't be dead, no."

My phone rang again, and it was my pastor's wife. Then it really kicked in that my friend was gone. I spent the whole day in denial that my friend was gone, but every time my phone rang, it was someone calling to give their condolences. I was told not to cry because I was pregnant and could put the baby in distress, but I couldn't help it. I couldn't suppress the pain.

A few days after my friend passed away, I felt disappointed, and my disappointment soon grew into anger: *God, I thought we prayed for her healing. We were expecting a miracle from You. We fasted and had faith that You would heal her from this cancer.* Because of my faith, however, I felt guilty for being angry, not understanding that the anger I felt was normal. I did write down how I felt in my journal—I was afraid of being judged for being angry with God. That was my outlet. It was my way of grieving and having healing conversations with God.

Anger is part of the healing process. It is an indication of how much love you had for the person. When you think of being angry, it can be intimidating; however, if you suppress, it will take longer for it to dissipate and for you to heal.

Anger can be aimed toward friends, the doctors, your family, yourself, the loved one who has died, or even God Himself. As believers, we often internalize that we shouldn't question God, but I believe it is healthy to ask God questions. It is a way of bringing to Him your anger, pain, and all the emotions stirring inside you. In this way, you actually have a conversation with Him, inviting Him to respond, but it is up to you to stand still to hear Him speak.

Guilt

Guilt is also a very common reaction to loss. It is a normal phase of grieving, but some people don't realize that. People often experience guilt because they feel as if they did not do enough for their loved one before they passed away, or they assume the blame for the death of the loved one. Guilt can be quite daunting to a person who was part of the tragedy that took someone's life.

If you are stuck in the phase of guilt, God wants you to know that "there is therefore now no condemnation for those who are in Christ Jesus" (Rom.

8:1 ESV). Condemning yourself won't change the tragedy; you have to release this guilt that's hanging over your head. Guilt can manifest into another unwanted emotion and stop healing in its tracks. Once you let go of this guilt, however, you allow yourself to move forward in the healing journey.

Depression

The loss of a loved one, home, or job is a very depressing situation. Intense sadness can fill a depressed person's heart. Depression is one of the most difficult stages of the grief process; it can lead to isolation and a debilitative state of mind. It is, however, an appropriate response to loss, and it is important that we recognize the signs of depression.

Even though some depression is normal during the grief process, some people might fall into a severe depression. If that happens to you, please don't shut out the support that's being extended to you. It's okay to seek professional help. It is important to be able to come to terms with your loss.

Acceptance

In chapter 3, I spoke about facing truth, and in the grieving process, acceptance is the final stage. That's the stage that will allow your heart to yield to healing. Once you have come to terms with the loss of a loved one, restoration doesn't feel so far away.

Acceptance does not mean that you have finished grieving or agree with what has happened; it simply means that you have accepted the reality. Readjustments and reorganizing roles come with acceptance.

You can never replace your loss, but as you begin to let go and move on, don't believe the lie that you're betraying your loved one. Coming to terms with acceptance may just mean having more good days than bad ones. You may move in and out of the grieving process; just keep including God in it and He will give you the guidance and peace you need to live again.

GOD WANTS YOU TO UNLEASH YOUR FEELINGS

«Why Have You Forsaken Me?"

As you know, anger is one of the stages of the grieving process. There are times that we aim our anger toward God. The feeling of abandonment and being forsaken may be present. Some people might ask, "Where is God in this?" or "How could He let this happen?" Matthew's Gospel shows that Jesus felt forsaken. When He was crucified on the cross, He cried out, "Eli, Eli, lema sabachthani?" which means, "My God, my God, why have you forsaken me?" (Matt. 27:46). He was innocent yet mistreated for His loyalty to God's will in His life.

Loss is very scary for some people, and it can leave them feeling as though God has forsaken them. Some theologians explain that it was Jesus' intent to quote Psalm 22:1[11]—"My God, my God, why have you forsaken me?"—to direct His bystanders to Psalm 22[12] so they would see the many fulfilled prophecies.

While theologians highlight the possible reasons for Jesus quoting Psalm 22, I see Jesus expressing His agony, unleashing His true emotions, and prophesying how you and I would react when facing despair. God wants us to unleash our feelings, despair, and anger and bring our questions to Him. Sometimes, however, we suppress how we're truly feeling in order to protect His feelings. He's not asking you to protect His feelings; He wants those who are weary and burdened to come to Him. He will not

---

[11] Larry White, "Why Jesus Cried 'My God, My God, Why Have You Forsaken Me,'" Bible Study Tools, November 25, 2019, |PAGE|, https://www.biblestudytools.com/bible-study/topical-studies/my-god-my-god-why-have-you-forsaken-me.html).

[12] "'My God, My God, Why Have You Forsaken Me,' Didn't Jesus Already Know?" interview, *Ask Pastor John* (audio blog, https://www.desiringgod.org/interviews/my-god-my-god-why-have-you-forsaken-me-didnt-jesus-already-know).

be intimidated by how you're feeling. Let God detox those toxic emotions.

> *Come to me, all you who are weary and burdened, and I will give you rest. Take my yoke upon you and learn from me, for I am gentle and humble in heart, and you will find rest for your souls. For my yoke is easy and my burden is light.* (Matt. 11:28–30)

TIME OF REFLECTION

- What are the stages of grief?
- Are you stuck in one or more of the grieving stages?
- Have you included God in your grieving journey?
- Take a moment to think about how your loss has affected you and how you can move forward.

Lord,

I have experienced loss; it is a very scary thing to experience. I want to unleash the emotions that have come with my loss experience. Remind me that You haven't forsaken me and that You're always with me. Teach me how to trust You in dark seasons. You know my heart and my thoughts. I don't want to hide my emotions. Heal my broken heart; my heart is Yours.

Feel free to express to Him what's on your mind.

10

CYNICAL LIFE

I grew up in a Christian household. My mother is a woman of great faith; she made us pray for everything—and I mean everything! As I grew older, I recognized the importance and power of prayer. There were areas in my life where I prayed and saw God move, and witnessed how He answered my prayers.

Nonetheless, during my quiet time with God, He recently showed me that I've been hosting cynicism in my mind for many years. There are certain areas in my life that I completely trust Him with, but when it comes to praying for someone's physical health, I don't want to pray. At times, I have rolled my eyes and huffed and puffed before starting a prayer, silently thinking, *Here we go again, God. I'm attempting to pray for healing for this person.* I would become anxious and question whether or not He would even heal. This reaction stemmed from all the sick people I had prayed for who yet passed away. I was afraid to question God about this because I had been taught not to question Him. Consequently, I buried my questions and disappointments.

I had heard stories of people getting healed from cancer and other illnesses doctors said were nearly impossible to cure, but when it was time for me to pray for physical healing, I would say, "I have faith, but . . ." God began showing me He needed to heal the cynicism that was robbing my hope for physical healing.

Can He Even Heal My Heart?

You may be broken, shattered, and just completely lost. I don't know what led you there; perhaps you've been through a divorce, the loss of a loved one, or even experienced betrayal from your significant other. There are many factors that can leave you at a place of brokenness. These series of experiences can cause you to become cynical, doubting what God can do in your life. Yes, God can heal your heart if you give Him access and are ready to listen to what He has to say to you.

Conquering Cynicism

Cynicism and faith can't grow in the same garden. That will prohibit you from seeing the work of God's hands. Cynicism is rooted in bad experiences and disappointments, and it loves company. For instance, if someone has a poor relationship with their earthly father due to broken promises he made, that person will be more skeptical of the promises their heavenly Father makes to them.

Listed below are some ways to conquer cynicism:

1. The best way to conquer cynicism is to *consistently* bask in God's presence. Seek His face, not His hand. If you consistently spend time with Him, you will rediscover the God who provides, heals, protects, and comforts, as well as recognize the many other wonderful traits He possesses.

2. Reinforce your faith instead of your negative thoughts. Surround yourself with a community that will help you reinforce your faith. See, cynicism is contagious if you're surrounded by people who are cynical; their cynicism will only reinforce your own cynical thoughts.

3. Take rest in God's knowledge and not your own. "'For my thoughts are not your thoughts,

neither are your ways my ways,' declares the Lord" (Isa. 55:8). When you pray for something, God knows the trajectory of your life. He answers, but it might not be the way you want. His knowledge, however, is far greater than yours. You just have to trust Him.

He said to them, "Because of your little faith, for truly, I say to you, if you have faith like a grain of mustard seed, you will say to this mountain, 'Move from here to there,' and it will move, and nothing will be impossible for you." (Matt. 17:20 ESV)

TIME OF REFLECTION

- Are you struggling with cynicism? If so, what experience led you there?
- Have you expressed your disappointment to God?
- What would you like to say to Him?

Father,

I ask You to forgive my cynicism. It has misguided me and blocked me from making connections with You and the plans You have for me. Despair and doubt have taken the form of cynicism in my life. I need a breakthrough from this mindset; open the floodgates of heaven and reign over my mind. I want to be free and conquer cynicism. I can't do this alone. Please take the lead, and I'll follow You.

Feel free to share your own prayers.

11

BURIED MEMORIES

I've met some people who said they intentionally buried traumatic experiences in their lives. No one wants to dwell on painful memories; it seems easier to shut down our emotions and not feel anything at all. However, the hard truth is, if you avoid this pain, it will show up in other areas of your life. You need to express the hurt inside you and then execute the pain so you can walk into your new life.

Opening old memories is actually good. You may find it difficult to remember what happened or don't understand the logistics, but this is where you invite the Holy Spirit to help you recollect the memories and awaken the life you're destined to live. Ask the Holy Spirit to give you understanding of what happened in the past. You will certainly be vulnerable, but He won't leave you feeling helpless. God will help you get to the root of the issue when you choose to do so.

What are the signs of buried traumatic memories?[13]

- Having strong emotional reactions to people who remind you of the negative experience
- Experiencing fear of certain situations or specific places
- Finding it difficult to gain control of your emotions

7. in order to maintain healthy relationships

- Having foggy memories of your childhood
- Struggling with addictions or impulsiveness
- Constantly emotionally exhausted
- Experiencing anxiety
- Possessing poor anger-management skills

The average number of days a woman spends in the hospital after giving birth is two or three days. After I gave birth to my son, however, I spent seventeen days in the hospital. I kept spiking fevers, and

---

[13] Carolyn Steber and Kaitlyn Wylde, "Experts Explain Signs of Repressed Childhood Trauma," *Bustle*, April 17, 2017, |PAGE|, https://www.bustle.com/wellness/signs-you-might-be-re-pressing-negative-childhood-memories-51958).

my heart rate was really high. I had all kinds of doctors asking questions, such as had I traveled outside the country? They also asked for my family's medical history. They ran many tests, scans, and X-rays in an effort to discover what was causing the fevers. The symptoms of an infection were evident, and several antibiotics were administered to me through an IV, yet the fever wouldn't subside. It was frustrating because the doctors couldn't get to the *root* of my health issue.

Many people have been, or are in, a similar physical situation because of an emotional aspect. Anger, depression, anxiety, and other emotions can be symptoms of a traumatic experience. These symptoms can be emotionally and even physically debilitating. If the root of the problem is not discovered, the problem will be treated with the wrong things.

Learn from It

In chapter 3, I spoke about the need to face the truth. Opening old memories is necessary in order to do this. That's where you will learn important life lessons to take with you into the next chapter of your life. Use these lessons as tools in your next journey. When you look at this as a learning experience, you make room for growth. Make the choice to work through these memories and process them fully. It is not going to be easy, but the outcome will be worth it.

When I was four years old, I was molested. I didn't really understand what was going on, but I was aware my body felt different. I never said anything to anyone until I was in the sixth grade. Then my best friend shared what had happened to her, and she used the word *molested.* I didn't know that word until she used it in that context. That's when it clicked for me—*So that's what happened to me.* I remember leaving school feeling angry yet sad that this had happened to me at such a young age. I didn't know who to speak to about it, so I buried the emotions and became numb.

When I wrote in my grief journal, that was the first thing I wrote about. I asked the Holy Spirit to help me open up this old memory. I was so afraid to feel and actually process what happened to me when I was four years old. I sat in my dorm room and closed my eyes; then I saw the vision of four-year-old me. I saw a scared and confused face, and I even remembered the sensation I had felt. As I began to process what had happened, I wept. I prayed and wept some more; all the emotions that I had shut down washed over me like an avalanche.

From this experience, I recognized that this adult had cultivated a friendship with me and then took advantage of it. That caused me to be skeptical of having new friends and made me wonder their potential agenda with me. I also realized that I had trust issues with men, and whenever I began a new relationship, I always wanted to feel protected.

As a parent, I now know how to speak to my children about molestation. I've also been able to speak to women who have been molested but have never spoken about it until I prayed with them. I know this is something I had no control of. Writing in the grief journal enabled me to evict anger, sadness, and perversion. If you have been molested, I pray you really take the time to release the emotions that have stemmed from your experience.

I want to affirm and declare some words that will help detox you and cultivate the person God calls you to be: You are not a mistake, and you can overcome this. You are not alone. It's okay to feel. If you're feeling guilt, know it was not your fault. You can be set free. Grace, peace, joy, and love are for you. God is able to restore everything the devil has stolen from you.

I pray that out of his glorious riches he may strengthen you with power through his spirit in your inner being. So that Christ may dwell in your hearts through faith. And I pray that you,

being rooted and established in love...
(Eph. 4:10)

TIME OF REFLECTION

- Think about the memories you may have buried.
- How are they affecting your current life?
- What lessons can you learn from the memories that you have buried?

Holy Spirit,

I invite You into a place where I've been wounded. I desire to move forward with my life, but I understand I've buried some things that are emotionally painful. Help me retrieve those memories and properly execute them. Holy Spirit, give me the capacity to deal with what I have buried. Allow me to feel what I have been too numb to feel. I want to be free from what's holding me back from experiencing Your presence. Thank You for loving me and wanting the best for me.

Feel free to say what's on your heart.

12

Are You Ready to Get Well?

I n Jesus' day, there was a pool in Jerusalem called Bethesda, meaning "house of mercy." Many disabled people used to lie there because from time to time, an angel of the Lord would stir the waters. The first person into the pool after the water was stirred would be cured of whatever disease or disability they had.

Among the people lying there was a man who had been a paralytic for thirty-eight years:

"When Jesus saw him lying there and learned that this man has been in this condition for a long time, he asked the man, 'Do you want to get well?'"

"'Sir,' the invalid replied, 'I have no one to help me into the pool when the water is stirred. While I am trying to get in, someone else goes down ahead of me.'"

"Then Jesus said to him, ‹Get up! Pick up your mat and walk.' At once the man was cured; he picked up his mat and walked" (John 5:6–9).

OFTEN, WE MISS OUR BLESSING BECAUSE WE'RE FIXATED ON GOD'S *PRESENTS* MORE THAN HIS *PRESENCE*

Presents Versus Presence

Now let's feast on the story of the paralytic man. What do I mean by *feast?* I mean let's **F**ocus, **E**ngage, **A**ssess, **S**park, and **Tune** in the story to see how can it apply to our lives.

First, this man had been paralyzed for thirty-eight years. So many questions may come to mind about this man: Where was his family? Did he have any friends? What type of emotions did he go through during the time he was paralyzed? Jesus asked him, "Do you want to get well?" Of course this man wanted to get well! However, his eyes were fixated on the pool and not having anyone to help him get in.

Often we miss our blessing because we're fixated on God's *presents* more than His *presence*. The paralytic man's response to Jesus wasn't a complete yes or no; it was an excuse, or more like a complaint. He stated the reason why he wasn't healed. He'd been lying on his mat and around disabled people for so long he knew only one way to get cured. The pool of Bethesda could have easily been considered a present to those who benefited from it. As long as the paralytic man *focused* his eyes on this present, he didn't grasp the eminence of the presence of Jesus standing before him.

When I read this story, I wondered why Jesus would ask this man, "Do you want to get well?" Then I had what Oprah calls an "aha moment." Perhaps Jesus wasn't referring only to this man's physical body, but also to his mind. This man had been paralyzed for thirty-eight years. His mind, most likely, was conformed to his circumstances and the circumstances of the other disabled people around him. His spirit was just as disabled as his physical body.

Blind, lame, and paralyzed people had surrounded him for many years. This man's perception of healing had been tainted, and he had been deceived by his physical condition. In those thirty-eight years, this man may have experienced disappointment, loneliness (even though he was surrounded by people like him), abandonment, self-pity, envy, and many other emotions that may have clouded his vision to see what Jesus was offering him.

Second, Jesus *listened*. The paralytic man's response revealed his spiritual paralysis. As the man spoke, I can only imagine what Jesus was thinking. Maybe He thought, *He doesn't know who I am, but I am about to change his life forever.* Jesus was fully aware of the man's condition, but He took time to listen before reacting to him.

Third, Jesus gave the man a *command*: "Get up, pick up your mat, and walk." Moreover, after Jesus' command, the man obeyed; he got up, picked up his mat, and at once was healed. The man's *faith* and *obedience* led him to healing. He could have stayed on his mat and complained about his aches and pains, but instead, he got up. The first few steps he took quickly reminded him, *This is my new normal, and I have to accommodate to it.*

Many times people don't want to speak to God because they think He's not listening. But Jeremiah 29:12 says, "Then you will call on me and come and pray to me, and I will listen to you." That's a given fact. He will listen to you when you speak; don't believe that He won't. Just as you expect Him to listen, He also expects the same from you. That's part of being obedient.

I've sometimes heard people express their disappointment over not hearing from God after they've prayed. Chances are, He spoke, but they didn't stop to listen because they were too distracted to receive what He said. When you miss out on what God has spoken, you miss instructions, commands, and directions. «Pick up your mat and walk." What is God commanding you to pick up? Is it blame, guilt, fear, hate, or rejection? You know deep down inside that the "mat" you have been resting on is crippling your mind, and God is telling you to pick it up and walk.

Faith is another component necessary for emotional healing. Yes, writing to heal is the main goal of a grief journal, but if you don't have faith that God will manifest healing for your brokenness, you're just writing to recollect pain that has weighed you down.

Walking in faith, however, fuels obedience. For example, if you have a strained relationship with your parents and haven't spoken to them for years, after writing about it in your grief journal, you may feel God prompting you to call them. It will require faith to believe that this is what God wants you to do, and it will take obedience to actually do it because this might be something you don't necessarily want to do. Nonetheless, you trust that He knows what He is doing, and you obey.

Her Story

When I was a student at Nyack College, an amazing service took place on November 7, 2007. Toward the end of the service, many students took some time to worship and pray. One student in particular was shouting and praising, "Oh my God, oh my God!" as she paced and ran back and forth.

I had seen this student on campus many times before, and we had engaged in small talks here and there. She always had a smile on her face. During the service, she was overwhelmed with joy, but it didn't occur to me something special was manifesting at that moment.

The next day she shared her story. She explained that she had been healed from cerebral palsy at the service the night before. She was amazed by how it happened, and her life was changed within a matter of minutes. She was completely blown away by this miracle.

As she shared her story, it hit me why she had paced and shouted—Jesus had healed her! I realized her posture was now completely different. As she spoke, she said something that resonated with me. It was simple yet powerful: "I have to throw all of my shoes away. I have to buy new shoes!" See, she had spent most of her life struggling with her balance, posture, and, overall, her mobility. She had to wear special shoes, and due to her posture, her shoes became deformed. I was completely blown away by her statement. Her body was healed, and her mind had to adjust to the new normal and accommodate her new posture.

While I was in the process of writing this book, I thought of her story. One day as I walked through downtown Brooklyn, I heard someone call my name. I looked over my shoulder, and lo and behold, it was that student God had healed from cerebral palsy. I was so happy to see her, as it had been seven years since I last saw her. We spoke briefly, then parted ways. As she walked away, I watched her. I was amazed for two reasons. First, I was amazed at God's timing because she had crossed my mind that week as I wrote the outline to this book. Her name was written on my outline. Second, I was amazed to see the difference in her walk.

What's Your Story?

Picture this: Jesus is standing before you, and He knows that your heart has been broken for many years. During those years, you have attracted people who are dealing with a broken heart as well, yet you and those people are lost and confused about the brokenness you all feel inside. Now Jesus hands a pen and paper for you to draw a picture of the condition of your heart. You draw patches and different types of wounds, such as lacerations, punctures, and abrasions, to show the severity of your brokenness. Then He asks you, "Do you want your heart to be mended? Do you want to renew your mind?" What will your answer be?

CAN THAT HAPPEN FOR ME?

I understand you've been through some things that negatively affected your life and keep you from moving forward. Or maybe you have moved on, but the problem you thought you buried is following you into every new chapter of your life. Many of us have heard of miraculous signs and wonders from the Lord, yet we ask, "Can that happen for me?" The answer is yes. Just like the paralytic man and the student who was healed from cerebral palsy, God can heal you physically and emotionally. He wants nothing but the best for you, but you have to trust Him.

My question to you is, Do you want to get well? Let's dig deeper. Are you ready to have your heart mended? Are you ready and willing to renew your mind? Just as Jesus asked the paralytic man, what will your response be? Will it be, "Yes, but I can't let go of what happened to me. . . ." "I am too angry. . . ." "I tried, but . . ." "It's not fair. . . ." "I struggle with . . ." "I don't have the time." Or some may even say, "Well, there's nothing wrong me."

These are answers you might find yourself saying. The first step to emotional healing is to admit that something is wrong. While you're writing to heal, your goal is to understand there is a call to action that needs to take place. You have a story that needs to be shared that will help those who experience what you experienced. You have the opportunity to spread hope to the hopeless, but you must start the process of emotional healing and let it continue.

As you know, this book is designed to help cleanse the toxic thoughts that are in your mind and affecting your life. If toxic things are lingering in your mind, then your heart has certainly been affected as well. The heart and mind are different, yet they're connected. Sometimes they work together, and sometimes they work against each other. For example, you may have heard it said, "My mind is saying one thing, but my heart is saying something else." Both heart and mind are needed in the process of emotional healing.

Peel Off the Label

The paralytic man was in his condition for thirty-eight years. It was part of his identity. In the NIV Bible translation, he is labeled as an "invalid." Can you imagine how someone might have given directions to the pool of Bethesda? "Go straight ahead and you will find an *invalid* man lying by the pool." For many years, this was the label and identity he had known. However, when Jesus told the man, "Pick up your mat and walk," he was immediately healed. The man was no longer an invalid. His new identity no longer matched the label he had carried for so many years.

YOU ARE NO LONGER WHAT YOU'VE BEEN LABELED

Your story is unique, and it is part of your identity. Through the healing process, you will have to peel off what other people or you have labeled yourself. We all have been labeled, whether it is "fat," "whore," "convict," "abused," "raped," "crazy," "stupid," "addict," "drunk," or something else. I want you to peel off those negative labels because you no longer have to assume they are permanent. You are no longer what you've been labeled. I don't know who has labeled you. It could have been your parents, a teacher, a counselor, a coach, friends, or even people from the church. Whoever it was, you can't allow their words to overpower what God has called you.

Jesus instructed the paralytic man to pick up his mat and walk. I spent many weeks asking God, "Why didn't Jesus just tell the man to get up and walk? Why did this former paralytic man need to take his mat with him?" He had been bound to it for so many years. If it were me, I wouldn't want to take it with me. I would want to break free from something I had been bound to for so long.

Recently, while I was reading the story of Joshua crossing the Jordan River with the Israelites, God answered my questions. See, the Israelites crossed on dry ground because God had dried where the river had been. When the nation crossed the Jordan River, God commanded Joshua to have twelve men from each tribe take twelve stones from the riverbed and carry them to their new destination. These stones were intended to be memorial stones, so that when future generations asked about the stones, the Israelites would share the history of the work of God on their behalf. The mat for the former paralytic man may have been a memorial for him, just as the stones were for the Israelites. God wants people to remember and share their stories with others. Allow this grief journal to be something you learn from, and share with those who need to hear it.

When I was in elementary school, there was a popular phrase that said, "Sticks and stones may break my bones, but words can never hurt me." That may sound great and help some people not to accept hurtful words said to or about them, but the reality is, words do hurt, and they can take root and grow.

I've seen people with a fractured bone recover faster than someone who has been hurt by words or labels used against them. You have to come to a place where you understand and accept what God has called you and how He sees you. While many people look at the outside, He looks at the heart. First Samuel 16:7 assures us of this. You don't have to adopt the labels that came with your life struggles. They don't define you. Through Christ, you have the power to remove the labels He didn't give you. You are victorious, redeemed, His masterpiece, and, last but not least, *you are loved.*

The mind usually refers to thoughts and intellect, while the heart refers to emotions, hopes, and other desires. Whatever is poured into your mind will trickle down to your heart. Perhaps all your problems are actually a heart-and-mind issue and you've misdiagnosed the problem. Even if you are a believer, it is possible to accept Jesus as your Savior yet still be miserable. Why? Because you haven't renewed your mind and dealt with your heart.

It is very easy to tell yourself and the people around you, «I'm fine, in the name of Jesus. God has me, so I'll just praise and shout my way through this." Yes, it is great to praise God when you're going through something. In fact, we're going to talk about that in chapter 13, so hang on. For now, however, I need you to understand the importance of verbalizing the pain and allowing yourself to grieve. If you don't, you may find yourself in the same place as the paralytic man who focused his eyes on the pool of Bethesda and thus did not recognize Jesus. You can't heal an unforgiving, angry, and abandoned heart with a shout, dance of praise, or a "God has me" declaration. That's just a pool of Bethesda you have focused on.

It is time to fix your focus on Jesus and magnify Him instead of trying to outrun your grief. Focus on Jesus, the one who can help you forgive and let go, to love and break free from fear, abandonment, and all the other issues that weigh your heart down. When you focus on Jesus, you magnify Him, and when you magnify Him, your brokenness begins to look and feel smaller.

It is always comforting to know that we have a friend who is just a phone call away when we're going through something. There's nothing wrong with calling a friend, but sometimes we immediately call our friend instead of going to God first. Don't get stuck in a wrong thought; the only way you can be healed is if someone helps you get into the pool of Bethesda.

> *I incline my heart to perform your statues forever to the end.* (Ps. 119:112 ESV)

I once heard a sermon by Pastor Steven Furtick about the habits of a healthy heart. He explained that real "lasting change has to happen in your heart."[14] Pastor Furtick also said that a mere change in behavior won't sustain the lasting change that you desire; it has to happen from within. How does it start from within? It happens when you acknowledge the condition of your heart and mind and then ask God for help. You have to make a choice to position your heart correctly.

Some things may have happened to you over which you had absolutely no control. They left you feeling a mess, and now you find yourself angry. Although you didn't have any control over past situations, you do have control over how you set your heart on God.

Think of the word *incline*. When I hear the word *incline*, I think of positioning on a treadmill. Oh yeah, I'm going to take it there. When you run on a treadmill, it is usually flat and parallel to the floor. However, if you want to challenge yourself and achieve better results, you incline the treadmill at an angle. In similar fashion, you must incline your heart toward God.

In Psalm 119:112, the psalmist expresses the inner issues of the heart. Many translations say "I incline," which means an intentional adjustment is made to the heart. The psalmist positioned his heart

---

[14] Steven Furtick, Pastor, "3 Habits of a Healthy Heart" (address, Elevation Church), https://www.youtube.com/watch?v=NRM00dIOAts).

at an angle aimed toward God. Inclining your heart can be as intense as inclining a treadmill. Running on an incline activates muscles and increases your heart rate. When you incline your heart toward Jesus, He helps you see circumstances from His perspective. He also activates your strength and endurance for the next situation that may occur in your life.

At the beginning of each new year, the gyms are packed. Many people are there because they have made a New Year's resolution to lose weight or become healthier. While the new members are occupying the exercise machines, the regular members are wondering how long this phase will last (for selfish reasons, of course). They have already gone through the process of discipline and commitment necessary to gym membership. Many times they will do a three-month countdown until the gym is not as crowded because they know some people will not stay committed to their New Year's resolution.

As for you, you have to stay committed to the healing process. Don't start and not finish. The outcome will be rewarding for both your present and your future. The psalmist said he inclined his heart to perform God's statutes forever, to the *end*. Don't let the process start and then lose your momentum. I encourage you to push through. You will face adversity, but don't allow it to change your heart's posture. As I mentioned before, even though you might not have control over life's adversities, you do have control over how you respond to them. You will have to make the act of renewing your mind a habit. Even when you face adversity, strive to incline your heart toward Jesus.

> *But seek first his kingdom and his righteousness, and all these things will be given to you as well.* (Matt. 6:33)

TIME OF REFLECTION

- Jesus wants to have an encounter with you. There's a call to action that's expected from you.
- Seek His presence, not His presents.
- Jesus wants to heal you. What or whom do you have your eyes fixed on?
- Jesus is commanding you to "pick up your mat and walk." Have you been comfortable lying on your mat?
- Are you ready for your emotional healing?
- Get your heart and mind in tune with each other.
- Incline your heart, and let it be lasting.

Dear Lord,

You know my thoughts and my ways. I have been trying to patch a wound that only You can heal. I've tried it my way and it hasn't worked out. Help me to seek more of Your presence rather than Your presents in my life. I want to magnify You and not my wounds. Give me the courage to pick up my mat and walk as You have instructed me. I don't want to complain anymore. I want to walk into the life that You have for me. Thank You for guidance, grace, and mercy.

Feel free to share your own prayers.

13

Your Goal

While you're planning or currently writing in your grief journal, you may experience a range of emotions. I pray that you find a trusted confidant or therapist to share about the process you're going through and the emotions you are feeling. You're taking a huge step to acknowledge the things that have had a negative impact in your life. This grief journal will help you reflect and receive revelations you need for the healing process.

> *Therefore, preparing your minds for action, and being sober-minded, set fully on the grace that will be brought to you at the revelation of Jesus Christ.*
> (1 Pet. 1:13)

WHERE THERE IS REVELATION, THERE'S ENLIGHTENMENT

Revelation About You

Writing in a grief journal is a practical principle to enhance receiving revelation about yourself. Although it is not the only way to achieve this, it is a good place to start. Where there is revelation, there's enlightenment.

As you begin to yield all your pain and concerns to God, He will reveal some things to you. You may not like some of it. In fact, you may find yourself wrestling with what He is revealing to you, but accept (obey) them anyway. Believe that He is revealing these things because He has great plans for you. Regard it as a privilege that He is giving you revelation. These revelations will help you deal with your pain more effectively. Remember, brokenness is painful and uncomfortable. The enemy will try to keep you in your brokenness because if you yield to God, you will fulfill His purpose.

Generational curses, toxic behaviors that have shaped your personality, and unwise decisions that have led you on a path of destruction may reveal themselves. It's time to stop using your zodiac sign to justify your toxic behavior. These things are toxic to your mind and your future. If God reveals cycles you keep getting sucked into, don't dismiss them. Continue to pray as you write in your grief journal, and allow your mind to be free from distraction so you can meditate on God's words.

JESUS UNDERSTANDS YOUR BROKENNESS

Beauty for Ashes

In this journey called life, you will face trials that will leave you broken. You may try to fix or forget about what happened, but maybe you're still living in pieces. But you don't have to live like that! Jesus understands your brokenness—He's been there. He sees the pieces you have tried to patch together. He has overcome the grave so that you can overcome the grave of toxic emotions, trauma, regret, shame, and betrayal.

> And provide for those who grieve in Zion—to bestow on them a crown of beauty instead of ashes, the oil of joy instead of mourning, and a garment of praise instead of a spirit of despair. They will be called oaks of righteousness, a planting of the LORD for the display of his splendor. (Isa. 61:3)

In biblical times, ash was associated with distress, loss, and suffering. It was customary for people to sit in or cover themselves in ashes after the death of a loved one or during great tragedies and trials to show their sorrow or repentance. Can you imagine that? The loss or trauma the person experienced led them to be covered in ashes. Now everyone knew they were hurting and mourning. There is nothing comfortable about that.

The nation of Israel was greatly oppressed, and they were taken into captivity. The political turmoil in the region was part of the reason they were oppressed. The people were afraid, confused, and, last but not least, felt that God had abandoned them.

We can relate to the Israelites, and like them, we can look to Isaiah 61:3 for hope and encouragement. Like the Israelites, you may feel afraid, confused, and abandoned, but remember what God says to you in Isaiah 43:5: "Do not be afraid, for I am with you." Your trials and difficulties may make you feel as though God has left you in the dark, but He hasn't. He will guide you through the darkness if you allow Him.

You might ask, «How can He guide me?" The answer is, through His Word: "Your word is a lamp unto my feet, and a light on my path" (Ps. 119:105). Allow God's Word to be a light unto your path. That's where you'll find beauty instead of ashes. Most of the time, however, we ask God to help us get out of the storm rather than asking Him to help us through the storm. Yes, of course, it may feel unfair that tragedy has struck you to the core of your soul, but God is in control. Trust Him.

We live in a time where we don't advertise our sorrows. We seem to be fine, but we're actually covered in ashes. Take a minute to think about the reasons you have covered yourself with ashes over the years. No matter what they are, God wants to take your trials and difficult situations and give you beauty in their place. He wants to anoint you with oil so the ashes in your life can dissipate, and He wants to make something beautiful out of your situation. Peace, freedom, love, and joy are beautiful, and that's what Jesus wants to give you. He sees your tossing and turning at night, your crying yourself to sleep, and He understands the loneliness you've been feeling even when you're surrounded by other people.

God cares about every area in our lives, and He wants us to give it all to Him. In our eyes, though, His plans may look outrageous. We may find ourselves asking, "God, why me? Why did this happen to me?" He wants us to trust Him, as Proverbs 3:5 says: "Trust in the Lord with all your heart and lean not on your own understanding; in all your ways submit to him, he will make your path straight." Many of us are so broken in spirit that out of desperation, we have created our own paths in an effort to find healing, instead of trusting God to heal our brokenness. It is time to live in His peace and not just exist in a world that is broken. There is more to your existence on this earth.

Oil of Joy

As I was reading Isaiah 61:3, "oil of joy" stood out to me. Why would Isaiah say "oil of joy" instead of just using the word *joy?* Perhaps he wanted the Israelites to understand that just as physical oil is hard to remove, the oil of joy would also be difficult to remove from a person's life. The Holy Spirit is often depicted as oil in the Bible. Moreover, oil in the Bible also symbolizes the Holy Spirit's anointing.

Have you ever seen an oil spill? Oil is one of the hardest substances to remove. If oil spills on a shirt, chances are, that shirt is ruined. God wants to exchange your mourning for the *oil of joy.* He wants to remove despair, anxiety, depression, and confusion in your life. You might be choking on ashes of bitterness, guilt, anger, or disappointment and feel as if you have no strength to fight for your emotional healing. God, however, wants to give you the oil of joy. No matter what storm may come your way, the oil of joy will always be there to sustain you.

A Garment of Praise Instead of a Spirit of Despair

We live in a time where so many styles from the past are trending again. Everyone has a style they like when it comes to fashion, and many people express themselves through the fashion they choose. Some try to find their self-worth through designer labels, but there is a garment that is not tangible yet more precious than designer clothes, custom-made suits, or even a beautiful wedding dress. It's the garment of praise. God wants to give you a garment of praise! However, you have to make the choice to wear it in every season of your life.

DESPAIR CAN FEEL SO HEAVY ON THE HEART, BUT THE GARMENT OF PRAISE IS SO MUCH LIGHTER ON THE HEART

Over the years, you have faced crazy storms in your life, which may seem unfair. They might have left you in despair or even caused you to question whether or not God was still there. Your circumstances cut so deep that you programmed your mind to move on. Despair can feel so heavy on the heart, but the garment of praise is so much lighter. You're probably wondering, *How can I put on a garment of praise when I'm so weak and hurting or _____?*

(Insert whatever applies to you: angry, confused, disappointed.) You have to make a conscious choice to put on the garment of praise, and it may require you to dig deep for strength. The storms will come—that's inevitable—but don't wait for your break-through and healing before you put on a garment of praise. That's where the healing is, in the praise. When you praise God in your storm, the praise becomes a potent weapon against the enemy.

Remember in chapter 12 when I said you can't heal an unforgiving, angry, and abandoned heart with a shout, dance of praise, or a "God has me" dec-laration? Okay, I want to explain this a little more. So many people of faith avoid dealing with the root of their grief. This book, however, is designed to encourage grieving through writing. As you write in your grief journal, it will shed light on your circum-stances, and it might even show you the need to seek a professional therapist. Yes, yes, yes, you can talk to Jesus and a therapist too. No, you're not replacing Him if you talk to a therapist. No, it won't make you weak if you talk to a therapist. No, no, no, you're not rejecting Jesus. I strongly believe Jesus and therapy work hand in hand. God will give you a garment of praise for the spirit of despair, and therapy will give you the tools to manage your emotions and the gar-ment of praise.

There was a pastor who lost his child and was understandably distraught. He spent many months angry with God and questioning his salvation. Whenever he expressed his pain to God, he would hear God say to him, *Worship Me*, but he was too angry and hurt to worship. This pastor turned to other things to find solace, yet he always ended up at the same place, angry and hurt. He tried his best to refrain from worshiping because it didn't make sense to him to worship God when he had lost his child.

At last, he grew tired, and a spirit of despair overcame him. He gave up and decided to worship God. God had given him a garment of praise, but it took him a while to decide to wear it. He kept putting the garment in the back of his closet before he finally made the choice to put it on. Once he did, however, the feeling of despair no longer consumed him. He was able to see that God loved him and would give him peace through the storm he had to face. This pastor experienced a grief nobody should ever have to experience, but putting on the garment of praise marked a turning point in his recovery.

Grief has its moments. One day, you're fine, and the next, you feel like you're falling apart. Although you already have access to the garment of praise, therapy can help you manage the waves of grief. But you have to decide whether you want to wear a garment of praise *and* seek professional therapy.

> *I will bless the Lord at all times; his praise shall continually be in my mouth.*
> (Ps. 34:1 ESV)

As you know, this grief journal will not be a simple task. You will have to find courage to deal with the pain, but it's time to exchange your brokenness for God's peace. He wants to put you on the path to wholeness so you can heal the way He wants you to heal. The enemy, however, wants you to believe that you are beyond repair. He also wants you to believe that you are rejected, forgotten, and useless. You're far from that! If you allow Jesus into your broken heart, you will see that He can mend it. "Behold, I am making all things new" (Rev. 21:5). He can make your heart new if you give Him permission.

A Time for Everything

> *There is a time for everything, and a season for every activity under the heavens: a time to be born and a time to die, a time to plant and a time to uproot, a time to kill and a time to heal,*

> *a time to tear down and a time to build,*
> *a time to weep and a time to laugh, a*
> *time to mourn and a time to dance, a*
> *time to scatter stones and a time to*
> *gather them, a time to embrace and*
> *a time to refrain from embracing, a*
> *time to search and a time to give up, a*
> *time to keep and a time to throw away,*
> *a time to tear and a time to mend, a*
> *time to be silent and a time to speak,*
> *a time to love and a time to hate, a*
> *time for war and a time for peace.*
> (Eccles. 3:1–8)

As Ecclesiastes 3:1–8 says, there's a time for everything. These times can be thought of as seasons. Past seasons are meant to be released so that you can embrace the new season that will come your way.

You don't necessarily have to go through a storm in order to write in a grief journal. It is not only for those who have experienced something traumatic or are facing life's adversities. It is also beneficial to grieve transitions and past seasons in order to embrace the new seasons in your life.

For example, I grieved after I gave birth to both of my children. Though it was a joy to experience the connection with the child in my womb, I experienced severe morning sickness and had to put off a lot of things until I regained my strength. Through my grief journal, I was able to release emotions that I had stored during pregnancy. When I had my second child, I was able to reflect and receive revelation about the transitional experience of being a first-time mom with my son to becoming a mother of two. I learned so much about myself both times. I encourage you to write and detox your mind to prepare for the new seasons in your life.

Whole

What does *wholeness* mean? According to the Merriam- Webster dictionary, *whole* means "to be healed. "[15] During your time of reflection, you will face the truth about your brokenness, and your goal is to seek the Holy Spirit to make you whole again.

You might be wondering what wholeness looks like. In the biblical context, wholeness means to be well in your spirit, mind, and body. I've heard many Christians speak this phrase: "Jesus has made me whole again." They are referring to God doing a complete restoration in their lives. If someone commits a trespass against them, for the sake of their mind, they have learned to forgive and let it go. The paralytic man by the pool of Bethesda was physically

---

[15] *Merriam-Webster,* s.v. "whole," definition 1 a (3), https://www.merriam-webster.com/thesaurus/wholeness.

broken, yet in the King James Bible, when Jesus commanded him to get up, pick up his mat, and walk, it says "immediately he was made whole," referring to his body being cured, undamaged, and unbroken.

God's desire for us is to be whole. We also have that desire to be made whole. We want to be whole in body, soul, and spirit, but we tend to look for wholeness in the wrong places. It is impossible to be whole on our own. Salvation is the step to wholeness—believing in our hearts that God sent His Son Jesus to die for us and give us full life, establishing the path to wholeness.

Although I encourage you to write in a grief journal to heal from your past, keep in mind that it is not the writing itself that will heal you. When you invite the Holy Spirit to come in during the process of writing, He will heal you. You just need the faith of a mustard seed to be blown away by His presence.

> *For God so loved the world that He gave His one and only Son, that whoever believes in him shall not be perish but have eternal life.* (John 3:16)

A Sinner's Prayer

Since salvation is a step to wholeness and wholeness is something you desire, I want to offer you the opportunity to take this step. If you haven't accepted Jesus as your Lord and Savior, and you desire to invite Him into your heart today, I wrote a prayer for you if you don't know where to begin:

Dear Lord,

I spent most of my life trying to do life without You. I am aware that I'm a sinner and don't have the power to save myself. I invite You to live in my heart, and I am ready to receive Your salvation. I accept You as my Lord and Savior, and I will put my trust in You. I believe that You are the Son of God who came from heaven to earth to die on the cross for my sins. Thank You for your compassion and the gift of eternal life. Amen.

Wholeness after Mind-Full Detox

Emotional abuse, sexual abuse, physical abuse, the death of a loved one, divorce, rejection, abandonment, depression, insecurity, or even a doctor's prognosis can rob you of wholeness. There are many more factors I haven't mentioned, but whichever one you experienced, it broke you and made you feel damaged.

I encourage you to reach for wholeness and not to settle for less. Don't go halfway and not finish the journey. You will overcome your brokenness, but it is imperative to realize that you have to be healed by a power far greater than yourself. Wholeness will cost you. Be ready for God to ask you to give up some things and make sacrifices. He may ask you to let go of a toxic relationship, negative thoughts, and your mask. God is determined to heal you. How determined are you to receive His healing?

> *But the Advocate, the Holy Spirit, whom the Father will send in my name, will teach you all things and will remind you of everything I have said to you.* (John 14:26)

Balance

When someone is on a weight-loss journey, they mistakenly think the process to lose the weight is hard. But once the pounds begin to shed through consistency and discipline from a well-balanced diet and exercise, they realize losing the weight wasn't as complex as they thought. The real challenge comes when they reach their weight goal and have to learn how to maintain the weight. We can apply this principle to our emotional healing process. Finding balance after this journey is very important.

You can easily find your mind becoming cluttered with toxic emotions due to life's storms and people's trespasses against you. Moreover, between your work schedule, school schedule, and life's overall schedule, a lot of pressure can consume your mind. In your lifetime, your emotions may fluctuate between feeling great and feeling sad. You will need to make time to take inventory of your life. It is important to find the balance between your mind, body, and spirit. The storms will come, and people will hurt you, but you must learn how to honor (accept) what has come to pass and release the toxic emotions that came with it. Remind yourself that it is okay to cry, and it is certainly okay to feel so that you can grieve.

Don't dismiss your pain. Just because you're coping doesn't mean you're healed from the situation. Make it the norm to grieve; grieving regularly allows you to attach the right emotion to the adversity that comes your way. When you grieve regularly, you create a healthy balance in your emotional health. Additionally, you don't have to worry about your mind being filled to its capacity. Regular grieving leaves room for the Holy Spirit to renew your mind.

Writing in a grief journal may not be the only way to grieve. This may sound contradictory to the grief journal experience that I'm encouraging you to do; however, the true focus and desire is for you to heal emotionally. We are all wired differently and respond to adversity in our own way; therefore, find what works for you and invite the Holy Spirit to manifest where toxic emotions have affected you. You can also seek counseling. It's totally okay; it doesn't make you crazy. What's crazy is hosting toxic emotions and expecting to live proactively.

In 2005, Hurricane Katrina devastated New Orleans. Many of Katrina's survivors were left with no choice but to migrate to Texas to start a new life. Unfortunately, many of those people who migrated to Texas experienced Hurricane Harvey when it struck in 2017.

Many news anchors had the opportunity to interview the victims of Hurricane Harvey. One woman who was rescued from a roof was also a Hurricane Katrina survivor. She had to restart her life in Texas after Hurricane Katrina. The only possession she was able to recover from her flooded home in New Orleans was a Bible that she had received from her former church.[16] Twelve years later, she faced another hurricane, Harvey, yet she demonstrated much resilience. She forced herself to focus on the positive aspects of her situation.

Although full details on how she grieved after experiencing Hurricane Katrina were not provided,

---

[16] "Harvey Survivor Who Was Rescued from the Roof of Rebuilding: 'God Is Looking out for Me,'" interview by Catherine Thorbecke, ABC News, November 13, 2017, |PAGE|, https://abcnews. go.com/US/harvey-survivor-rescued-roof-rebuilding-god/ story?id=51104208).

she did express that she cried out to God after Hurricane Harvey. It was evident that her faith had increased her emotional capacity to handle another devastating hurricane.

It is important that we learn to release our pain and concerns to God; it helps to develop resilience. This woman's dream was to have a home of her own to raise her family. She gave herself permission to dream and rebuild.

I pray that you continually find balance after your mind-full detox journey so that you have the emotional capacity to face any storm life throws at you. Healthy grieving also leaves room for a grateful heart instead of self-pity. When practicing a heart of gratitude, you shift the focus onto positive thinking instead of what's lacking. Negative thinking can be very toxic.

> *Our failure to grieve can lead us to a state of paralyzing doubt in God and the people around us.* (Ron Walborn)

Lastly, stay in communication with God. Don't wait for a life crisis to hit for you to remember to pray. When your mobile device is running low on its battery, you connect it to a charger to raise the battery percentage. Don't treat your spirit like your mobile device; rather, stay connected to God.

In life, you will constantly experience emotions that can cause an imbalance. The Holy Spirit will teach you which ones to keep and which ones are toxic and need to be released. He wants to guide you through storms and mend what's been broken so you can live in the present and not your past. God also wants you to remain balanced with your emotions.

> «Return to your home, and declare how much God has done for you." And he went away, proclaiming throughout the whole city how much Jesus had done for him. (Rom. 3:19)

Storyteller

When you are finished with your grief journal, there is something I would love for you to see. I want you to recognize that you have a powerful story, and God wants to do something with it. There are so many people who have been in your place or will experience what you've been through. Your story needs to be heard. It will connect you with those who need to grieve. Your story will bring light and hope to those who need it. It will also remind you that through the power of the Holy Spirit, you overcame something that you thought you'd never be healed from.

You've made it through some trials and tribulations. You might have some elements that you're not proud of, but believe that your transparency will help set someone else free. For instance, a former drug addict's body might show track marks (needle scars), and the addict might cover them up due to shame, but this is actually a pivotal moment for both the former drug addict and a current drug addict. I have found that I am able to connect with people when I'm transparent about my life story. People are able to relate to me and are elated to know there's hope for them as well.

The enemy doesn't want you to share your story because he knows how powerful and effective it will be to others. He may try to distract you with fear and doubt, but there is someone who is waiting to hear how God moved and healed you emotionally. Someone out there needs to know how you used to avoid grieving, but now you've learned to grieve and heal. It's like a relay race where you're passing the baton to the next person, and that person will do the same for somebody else. God wants to use your story.

> *Sing praises to the Lord, who sits enthroned in Zion! Tell among the peoples his deeds!* (Ps. 9:11)

We are living in a world full of darkness, and your story has the power to bring light into somebody's world. The enemy has convinced many people that God is absent from their lives. Your story will show them, however, even though they are surrounded by darkness, God is very present and ready to help them. God's overall plan is for people around the world to hear the good news that Jesus paid the ultimate price for their sins and shame. He conquered the grave by rising from the dead. When they believe that, people will receive the power of the Holy Spirit. Your story can lead people to God's overall plan.

> *The man went away and told the Jewish leaders that it was Jesus who made him well.* (John 5:15)

Former Paralytic Man's Story

In the previous chapter, I shared the story about the paralytic man. The day Jesus commanded him to pick up his mat and walk was a Sabbath. When the Jewish leaders saw the man carrying his mat, they reminded him that the law forbade carrying a mat on the Sabbath. The man replied, "The man who made me well said to me, ‹Pick up your mat and walk.'" That moment marked the day this man became a storyteller. Although the Jewish leaders looked past what Jesus had done for him, he shared his story. Some people might not receive your story well, but don't let that stop you from sharing with those who need to hear it.

Picture this: You're washing your hands, and you remember the sink was once clogged, but now the water is flowing through the faucet and down the drain with ease. Now you're able to walk away in peace. Why? Because you took care of the underlying issue. You unclogged what was holding back your blessing.

Time of Reflection

- Do you understand what your goal is after you finish your journal?
- During your time of reading, what have you learned about yourself?
- Has the Holy Spirit revealed anything to you?
- Do you have a confidant or therapist to aid you through this process?
- Are you ready to be made whole again?
- Are you cultivating good habits to balance your emotional health?
- Be ready to become a storyteller!

*When the righteous cry for help, the
Lord hears and delivers them out of all
their troubles.* (Ps. 34:17)

Dear God,

*My help comes from You. I am ready to grieve and
allow You to show me the toxic emotions I need to
release. Help me keep my eyes on You. Give me the
strength to deal with feeling uncomfortable. Bring
peace to my anxiety. Thank You for loving me and
wanting nothing but the best for me. Amen.*

Feel free to say your own prayers.

ACKNOWLEDGMENTS

And we know that in all things God works for the good of those who love him, who have been called according to his purpose. (Rom. 8:28)

There are some things we experience in life that seem so unfair. We may get frustrated and question God's motives, but He knows what He is doing. I now can look back and simply thank God for the storms He allowed to come my way because I am able to see His glory and true love for me. I thank Him for leading me on this path and strategically ordering my steps.

Along this path God orchestrated for me, I have met some wonderful people. I met my husband, Reginald Regnier, whom I am truly thankful for. Our love story actually started off with us writing in grief journals. My husband took the Spiritual Formation class in college and was required to complete the grief journal assignment. I never took that class; however, my mentor, Pastor Kelvin, suggested that I write in a grief journal. I didn't want to do it at first, but God tugged at my heart to do so.

When I finally wrote in my grief journal, God told me that I would give it to my future husband. I thought this was bizarre, but lo and behold, when my husband, who was just my friend at the time, expressed his feelings for me, he said he had been writing in a grief journal. He said he wanted to share it with me, and I told him I had also worked on a grief journal. My husband suggested we exchange grief journals then burn them to symbolize the letting go of our past. This experience fueled us, and our love story began.

My husband is very supportive of my dreams and aspirations. I love his accountability, his affirmation, and the way he protects my dreams. He often says things like, "Yad, pray and make moves—you got this"; "I am proud of you"; "We are in this together." His words truly encourage me to keep moving on the path God has for me.

We have three beautiful children: Immanuel, Riley, and Faith. They are so young, yet I learn so much from them. When my son saw that I was working on a book, he told me he was proud of me and also affirmed me. Whenever I have my quiet time with God, my son lays his hands on me and prays for me.

My daughter Riley, when she was one year old and couldn't fully say a complete sentence, taught me to be resilient. She's rambunctious, a risk-taker, and often she gets hurt from taking a risk. She then says, "Ouch," and shows either my husband or me where she has hurt herself and needs us to kiss her boo-boo. Then she gets back on her feet and plays as if nothing has happened. Like my daughter, I have to take risks on my journey, and if I get hurt, I will take my pain to my heavenly Father.

Lastly, when I was pregnant with my last child, doctors had concerns she might have Down syndrome. At first, I was worried, then I learned to pray differently. Instead of asking God, "Why me?" I said, "Lord, prepare me for Your plans." I knew my way of thinking had changed as the result of grief journaling. «*Chemen sa pa fasil, toujou rete nan lapriyè*» is something my parents often said to my siblings and me. It means, "This path is not easy, but you have to stay in prayer." They embedded in us the necessity of praying at all times. I've learned to pray in good times and in bad times, and I thank my parents for teaching me the power of prayer.

To my siblings, who are very protective of me, I thank you for being there when things didn't make sense to me about the path God had placed me on. I love how you guys are willing to drop everything in a heartbeat to tend to me when I need your help. You guys are amazing!

On this path in life, my family has come across a wonderful church, Purpose Life Church, where we have met wonderful people who have become our church family. I want to thank my pastor and his beautiful wife, Pastor Heston and Lady Sharese. Thank you so much for being not only preachers but also teachers. You have taught me to live my life on purpose and love on purpose. Thank you!

I also want to thank our friend and mentor, Pastor Kelvin and his wife, Doni, who have always been there for my husband and me, telling us, "I dare you to dream big. You'll be alright." We appreciate you.

I have so many friends and family who have been with me on this path. I don't want to name you all because I might just miss someone, but you know who you are. I truly thank you for your prayers, advice, shoulders to cry on, wisdom, and, last but not least, your support. God has truly blessed me with each one of you. Thank you from the bottom of my heart.

BIBLIOGRAPHY

Calhoun, David B. "'Amazing Grace' John Newton and His Great Hymn." *Knowing & Doing*, no. Winter (November 22, 2013): 1–5.

Clarke, Jodi, MA. "The Five Stages of Grief." Very Well Mind. March 21, 2020. https://www.verywellmind.com/five-stages-of-grief-4175361.

Ehrenfeld, Temma. "Forgiveness Is Good for You." *Psychology Today*. November 3, 2016. https://www.psychologytoday.com/us/blog/open-gently/201611/forgiving-is-good-you.

Eltagouri, Marwa. "Acts of Faith." *Washington Post*, November 17, 2017. https://www.washington-post.com/news/acts-of-faith/wp/2017/11/10/why-this-father-hugged-the-man-who-helped-kill-his-son/.

Furtick, Steven, Pastor. "3 Habits of a Healthy Heart." Address, Elevation Church. https://www.youtube.com/watch?v=NRM00dIOAts.

"'Super Bug.'" Interview by Van Jones. CNN. January 27, 2018.

Marcin, Ashley. "9 Ways Crying May Benefit Your Health." HealthLine. September 14, 2017.

Merriam Webster. https://www.merriam-webster.com/thesaurus/wholeness.

Merriam Webster. https://www.merriam-webster.com/dictionary/repent.

Merriam-Webster Dictionary. https://www.merriam-webster.com/dictionary/intimacy.

"'My God, My God, Why Have You Forsaken Me' Didn't Jesus Already Know?" Interview. *Ask Pastor John* (audio blog). https://www.desiringgod.org/interviews/my-god-my-god-why-have-you-forsaken-me-didnt-jesus-already-know.

Steber, Carolyn, and Kaitlyn Wylde. "Experts Explain Signs of Repressed Childhood Trauma." Bustle. April 17, 2017. https://www.bustle.com/wellness/

signs-you-might-be-repressing-negative-childhood-
memories-51958.

"Harvey Survivor Who Was Rescued from the
Roof of Rebuilding: 'God Is Looking out for Me.'"
Interview by Catherine Thorbecke. ABC News.
November 13, 2017. https://abcnews.go.com/US/
harvey-survivor-rescued-roof-rebuilding-god/
story?id=51104208.

Walborn, Ron, Dr. "It's Ok to Cry." The Alliance.
September 16, 2016. https://www.cmalliance.org/
alife/its-ok-to-cry/.

White, Larry. "Why Jesus Cried 'My God, My God,
Why Have You Forsaken Me.'" Bible Study Tools.
November 25, 2019. https://www.biblestudytools.
com/bible-study/topical-studies/my-god-my-god-
why-have-you-forsaken-me.html.

NOTES

_____

_____

_____

_____

_____

_____

_____

_____

_____

_____

_____

_____

_____

_____

_____

_____

_____

_____

_____

_____

_____

_____

_____

_____

_____

_____

_____

_____

_____

_____

_____

_____

_____

_____

_____

_____

_____

_____

_____

_____

_____

_____

_____

_____

_____

_____

_____

_____

_____

_____

_____

_____

_____

_____

_____

_____

_____

_____

_____

_____

_____

_____

_____

_____

_____

_____

_____

_____

_____

_____

_____

_____

_____

_____

_____

_____

_____

_____

_____

_____

_____

_____

_____

_____

_____

_____

_____

_____

_____

_____

_____

_____

_____

_____

_____

_____

_____

_____

_____

_____

_____

_____

_____

_____

_____

_____

_____

_____

_____

_____

_____

_____

_____

CPSIA information can be obtained
at www.ICGtesting.com
Printed in the USA
BVHW050810070921
616214BV00013B/591

9 781662 825927